# Welcome to My Trading Room

# Welcome to My Trading Room

*Basics to Trading Global Shares, Futures, and Forex*

*Volume I*
*Foundation of Trading*

Jacques Magliolo

BEP BUSINESS EXPERT PRESS

*Welcome to My Trading Room: Basics to Trading Global Shares, Futures, and Forex, Volume I: Foundation of Trading*

Copyright © Business Expert Press, LLC, 2017.

First published in 2017 by
Business Expert Press, LLC
222 East 46th Street, New York, NY 10017
www.businessexpertpress.com

ISBN-13: 978-1-63157-875-5 (paperback)
ISBN-13: 978-1-63157-876-2 (e-book)

Business Expert Press Finance and Financial Management Collection

Collection ISSN: 2331-0049 (print)
Collection ISSN: 2331-0057 (electronic)

Cover and interior design by Exeter Premedia Services Private Ltd., Chennai, India

First edition: 2017

10 9 8 7 6 5 4 3 2 1

Printed in the United States of America.

# เคที ฉันรักคุณผู้หญิงบ้า

# Abstract

This Volume builds a foundation of knowledge in a comprehensive body of literature on trading to prepare the novice to become a professional trader. This volume starts with the total basics of trading with more in-depth knowledge being explored in the next two volumes.

# Keywords

AMEX, bears, bonds, bulls, futures, rules, index, IPO, LSE, NASDAQ, NPL, options, ords, OTC, Prefs

# Contents

# Author's Declaration

I, Jacques Magliolo, declare that I will:

- Set out easy to read and understand financial concept and trading methods.
- Offer readers direct access to my trading programs and mentorship.
- Provide readers with continuous research and information via financial and trading newsletters.
- Start with easy strategies and help you develop more complex systems in a building blocks basis, starting with the establishment of a solid foundation of knowledge and increasing that knowledge throughout these three volumes, to ultimately become a professional trader.
- I will teach and guide you to create a three-level portfolio.
  - The first will be your long-term trading portfolio, or also known as your retirement portfolio.
  - The second will be a medium-term trading portfolio, which is futures and hedging portfolio to take advantage of market noise and anomalies.
  - The third will be a day trading portfolio, which will enable you to generate a monthly salary.
  - The aforementioned must become habit and, consequently, your entrée to professional trader status.
- I will show you how to research, disseminate, and analyze information to trade with knowledge and discipline.
- I will show you how set up a trading journal and how to implement realistic and easy to use trading strategies.

These are my promises, but in turn, to become a successful trader you have to pledge the following:

- You will be diligent in conducting trades.
  - This means that you will gather knowledge about markets, sectors and shares before you conduct any trade.
- You will be disciplined and keep to your own strategies, which means that you will trade according to a predetermined set of self-created and developed rules.
- Trading without strategy is merely guesswork. You may succeed in numerous trades and it may be fun, but ultimately your career will be short lived.
- You don't have to trade every day; nobody is forcing you. That is, if the market does not meet your personal trading rules, stay out of the market. There are always market opportunities, so don't see lost trades, but rather concentrate on future opportunities.

Why do I ask you to make such a pledge?

Well, for starters, emotion plays a phenomenal role in a trader's long-term success or failure.

It is well documented that about 90 percent of the world's population work for the remaining 10 percent, which means that it is the norm to work for a salary by selling your services or professionalism for a minimum of 40 hours a week.

To change from this salary income base to one where you have to be self-sufficient in obtaining your salary takes discipline and knowledge.

For instance, imagine making losses 4 days in a row, or not trading for 5 days because market conditions were not conducive or too volatile and so on. The novice trader will start to think about his salary, which he or she now has to make up in the remaining 15 trading days of that month.

Panic often sets in and strategy is abandoned to favor of higher risk trades. A simple solution is to have a salary buffer of 6 months as part of your trading strategy. This way, you trade according to strategy and whatever the shortfall is at the end of the month you can draw from your money market account.

When you surpass your salary target, place the additional funds in your money market account. Remember that some months are more difficult to trade, such as holiday times and elections.

Understand that as the mundane regular job falls away, so too does a regular, normal, and safe income. This means that while your time may become your own, it also means that "no work, no pay" becomes all too often a cruel reality. Achieving this financial independence therefore comes with specific monitory management and properly planned goals.

You do not have a choice, but to take these goals seriously. Remember the following truism, which many novice traders fail to learn until it is too late:

- You do not have to trade every opportunity that comes your way.
- You do not have to trade every day.
- You do not have to trade every type of security available.
- Effectively, trade according to your level of knowledge and comfort. Stay focused and disciplined.

When you achieve the following simple basics:

- Ensure that you start slowly to build knowledge.
- Ensure that you are disciplined in your trading.
- Ensure that you are serious about this new "job." Going to work in your pajamas, or taking regular unnecessarily long lunches to not being prepared prior at the opening bell, is not being serious. Your attitude to success plays an extremely important part of your future success.

Stated differently, you need to master two basic habits to be a trader:

- The habit of being scrupulous in using a realistic set of rules or strategy to earn both a salary and a long-term retirement investment income.
- The habit of refining your strategies and researching how markets work. Essentially, you start investing and trading within your level of comfort, that is the country that you are most familiar with and then expanding that horizon as your knowledge grows. For instance, if you are an American trader,

develop your trading skills for the U.S. markets and then, over time, expand to trading emerging market stocks as your knowledge of how such markets work improves.

If you can acquire these two basic habits, you are certainly ready to start your journey to becoming a trader. The three volumes are thus set out to achieve the aforementioned; as follows:

- **Volume 1:** Basics of trading.
  - We start with an overview of how markets work, outlining different types of securities, and how they function in the market.
  - More importantly, though, is an outline of professionals' lessons about trading; outlining wisdoms from past and current market masters.
- **Volume 2:** Setting up your own brokerage.
  - An overview of critical structures for trading is established.
  - A more complex overview of markets and cyclical fundamentals is highlighted.
  - This volume is essential as a precursor to Volume 3.
- **Volume 3:** Combing fundamental and technical analysis.
  - This is the volume all novice traders have been asking for.
  - To succeed as a trader, you need to understand both fundamental analysis and how to use technical triggers.

The three volumes combine to give you an overview of markets, trading techniques, and strategies to succeed as a trader. If you need more techniques or understanding of how markets work, don't hesitate to send me a message.

**—Jacques Magliolo**
jacques@bci.za.com
www.bci.za.com
2017

# Foreword

*The market will be here tomorrow.*

This Volume is the culmination of an idea, which I had many years ago, to compile a comprehensive body of literature on trading; *from total basics to entering international markets.*

Consequently, these three volumes are just the start of this idea to effectively mentor novice traders while, at the same time, teach students and private clients the basics of trading and, then build depth of knowledge, skill, and experience. The aim is to write a number of books to cover the elements that make up sound trading techniques, from fundamental analysis to identifying corporate strength, to recognizing effective technical triggers to time securities trading; basics of investments through to setting up a strategy to trade for a living.

This idea germinated after I had completed a set of articles for a South African financial newspaper on share analysis and company forecasting. The series became extremely popular, for which I was grateful, but it was the indirect consequence of these articles that led me to taking my first step to writing a financial book. An elderly CEO of an international motor corporation phoned me and it is what he said that has had a direct result in these volumes being compiled and written.

The CEO: "Do you know how little boards of directors understand about markets, how they work, and what influences share prices?"

My first thought was that this was their problem, but on review it struck me that this CEO was making a point about the company's share price and only indirectly about his directors. So, he admitted, if directors know these factors affect their company's shares, then they could influence share price by improving investor sentiment.

I felt that, after seeing hundreds of companies with poor financial structures, and even worse management controls, result in appalling investor sentiment and thus declining share prices—he was making an extremely pertinent point.

Ultimately, the articles and the CEO's comments became my entrée into the world of corporate finance, stockbroking, and that of writing my first book, *Share Analysis and Company Forecasting* in 1995. *The Business Plan: A Manual for South African Entrepreneurs* was published the following year and became the business textbook at the University of Kwa-Zulu Natal in South Africa.

The next three financial books looked at issues that make up trading in a global and emerging market environment; including strategy, emergence of small capitalization stock exchanges, like the UK's AIM (Alternative Investment Market), Canada's TSX, and the South African Alternative Exchange (AltX) and the similarities between standard portfolio theory and entrepreneurial methodologies.

In 2003, *Jungle Tactics: Global Research, Investment & Portfolio Strategy* covered factors that influence businesses and portfolio investments in a global market, *A Guide to AltX* (2004) outlined the methodologies of how to prepare for listing on a small cap market and *Corporate Mechanic: The Analytical Strategist's Guide* (2007) set out methods to restructure a company to become efficient, profitable, and protected from the hostilities of international corporate raiders.

During the following years, I had left stockbroking to head up *Business Consulting International* and immediately noted two new corporate trends. First, entrepreneurship was becoming increasingly international, with cross-border business rising, and online trading was becoming extremely popular.

Consequently, I decided to write a book on global project management and *The Guerrilla Principle: Winning Tactics for Global Project Managers* was published in 2008 by Juta. This book was rated number two worldwide and was quickly followed by four books on trading methodologies, namely *Richer Than Buffett, Women & Wealth, Lore of the Global Trader and Master Trader.*

In 2013, I was commissioned to write and edit a book entitled *Business & Entrepreneurship*, for a South African business school.

When you work as a trader you will find that most of your time is spent researching, analyzing, and strategizing on market and industry trends and how determining trading ranges and fair value.

So, if you think that you will be glued to a screen, buying and selling shares for hours at a time, then you need to learn the first lesson of trading, which is that this is a professional industry and not a gambling arena. You trade based on preestablished rules and analyses. This doesn't mean that trading is boring, merely conducted in an organized and predetermined manner. Ultimately, experience combined with skill, knowledge, and discipline will push you into the professional status. But heed a warning, it is easy to become complacent and sloppy, ignoring your own trading strategies by chasing the market when profitable trends seem to be easy and winning seems obvious. This is the greed factor that leads many novice traders to go back to their day jobs.

# A Personal Note to All Novice Traders

These three volumes are for both beginners and professional traders and, as such, are aimed at providing you with the skills to set up and maintain your own portfolio of securities. My advice is always to start with shares and, when you have mastered this form of security, move onto derivatives, such as warrants, options, bonds, futures, commodities, and money market instruments. These will all help in the full diversification of risk and rewards should, by all accounts, be greater.

So, before you practice setting up your portfolio and building stock market skills, there is an essential first process for you to undertake. These volumes are comprehensive, but essentially success often comes in a three-fold approach to trading.

- **Understand the environment you are about to enter**. Once you understand the rules of investing, you can set up your portfolio. Once you have a basic understanding of how stock markets work and how you can trade, the second step is to create your own specific databases and the structures of a portfolio. So, once you have a portfolio, you have to acquire shares.
- **Set up your portfolio**. From gathering information to portfolio structures, from types of risks to strategies, these are all set out in this volume.
- **Strategies to trade**. You need a system to research shares, a means to identify winners and develop strategies to enter and exit trades.

If you are a beginner, I recommend following these steps. If you are a more experienced stock investor or trader, feel free to skip around to the steps of interest.

# PART I

# Demystifying Stock Markets

# CHAPTER 1

# The Enigma of Stock Markets

*As you gain experience, you can better plan your trades. Then trade this plan until you refine your strategy.*

## Start by Building a Foundation of Knowledge

Many years ago, when just starting out as an equity analyst, I discovered that many clients in general had a completely incorrect understanding of how stock markets work. Often I was asked if I was a stockbroker or a trader, and if I can buy XYZ shares for them? Tell me about this particular share, bond, or economic scenario for the next year?

The essence of a stockbroking firm is that it is just like *any other firm*. There are clerks, administrators, bosses, secretaries, divisions of traders, sales teams, and researchers. There are executive-director meetings, morning meetings, client visits, strategies, shareholders, and partners.

The importance to the novice trader is an understanding of the different types of positions that make up a broking firm. Not everyone is a stockbroker, nor is everyone a trader! The following section adopts a threefold approach.

- First, a general understanding of how stock markets work.
- This is followed by a brief breakdown of how a stockbroking firm operates.
- Finally, a brief description of securities available through stock exchanges.

## Defining Stock Markets

Watching people throw their arms up, wave, yell, and signal to each other on stock exchanges around the world can be very intimidating to beginners.

Called the *Open Outcry System*, these have mostly been replaced by electronic trading systems around the world, which is even more intimidating and it is extremely difficult to imagine how the market works in all that chaos. You need not worry, it really is not that complicated.

### Time to Demystify Stock Exchanges

The fact is, most people do not truly understand what a share actually is or what it means to trade shares. Contrary to what many think, the stock market is not there to get rich quickly.

Stock markets are just that—markets. In this case, a market to facilitate in an organized manner the exchange of shares between buyers and sellers. Just imagine how difficult it would be to sell shares if you had to call around to friends, neighbors, or total strangers and attempt to find a buyer. So, just think of exchanges as sophisticated methods of linking buyers and sellers from anywhere in the world.

The mechanism is relatively basic. A company that needs cash flow goes to the exchange and asks the public for money to help it in its venture. To obtain these funds, the owner effectively sells a part of his company to these many investors. They do not actually break up the company, but supply the investor with a piece of paper (share certificate or, as is the case in modern exchanges, an electronic share certificate number), which certifies that he or she owns a stated number of share in a specific company. It must be noted that these certificates are disappearing in modern exchanges, being replaced under a "dematerialization" of share certificates, which are effectively being swopped for electronic numbers to facilitate a quicker exchange of shares. It also makes way for quicker payment for shares, as no certificates have to be issued.

This type of electronic share certificates is the future face of trading around the world. The system effects settlement for both share transactions on the exchange and for off-market trades. The norm in the world of trading is that it takes 3 days for the exchange to transfer to you funds received from the sale of shares. This is called T+3.

The result of electronic trading has been an increase in trading volumes, which also highlighted the deficiencies in the paper-based settlement system. Ultimately, the screen-based system contributes to a significant rise in daily trading turnover. For example, in 1990, the daily trading volume on the JSE was R5 million, and today it is over R1 billion.

**Let me reiterate.** The stock exchange is *just* a market place. It is a place where people who want to buy shares can meet with people who want to sell them—through a stockbroker. A stockbroker's job is to bring the seller and buyer of a particular share together, using computer systems. Buyers and sellers just phone their broker and tell him how many of what share they want to buy or sell. Or, with online trading, traders can execute trades via an online trading platform.

The broker then executes the transaction (usually within the next few minutes) by entering it onto the computer system. The online trading platform is continuously searching for those buyers and sellers of any particular share that can agree on a price. As soon a price suits both the buyer and the seller, the transaction is instantly and automatically completed.

Transactions can also be placed electronically over the Internet with most broking firms.

### Get Your Part of a Listed Company

A share is a part ownership of a company. All companies have shares—but the only ones which we are interested in are the ordinary shares of public companies that are listed on an exchange. If you look at the price page of newspapers or online trading websites, you will see that these companies are grouped into "sectors," mostly according to what industry they are in.

Each of these companies has a quantity of "issued shares"—meaning shares which have been sold to members of the public (in the primary market) in exchange for the money needed to start or expand the company.

Once you own shares, you can then trade these in the market, that is sell the shares to unknown buyers and use the funds to buy shares in other listed company shares; this time from unknown sellers.

Take note that electronic trading systems match buyers and sellers on price, but also on volumes of shares to be traded. This means that you may only get some of your order.

These transactions take place in the secondary market and have no direct impact on the company itself. If the company is perceived to be profitable and growing then the shares should rise in value—and, if not, then the share price could fall. You should also note that I use the words *should* and *could* as share prices move on two fundamental principles; namely the company's financial health and investor and trader sentiments. These traders may or may not be informed, educated, and experienced enough to evaluate the company correctly—and, even if they are, they will usually have different opinions about what it is worth.

So, investors effectively own a portion of the company to the extent of the shares they hold, for example, if James buys 10 percent of all shares issued by the company, he then owns 10 percent of that company. For his part ownership he may receive, at the directors' discretion, an interim and an annual dividend payment (compared to a bank interest rate). Of course, the more he owns, the greater his control of the company.

As markets developed, investors were able to sell these shares to other investors and thus the exchange has a dual purpose. Not only were companies able to acquire funds, but the public has another means of investing directly into a company's growth.

Another way to define stock markets is as a forecast or precursor of future general economic activity. Exchanges are thus systems that promote public participation in the economic decision-making process through their ownership of corporations listed. As a consequence of investors' freedom to choose shares, they indicate how national resources can be better utilized.

Conclusion: The stock market is the leading indicator of economic performance of a country.

Let me explain it. Exchanges tend to have the largest companies in a country as listed entities. Therefore, as these companies start to earn higher profits, their employees tend to benefit from higher wages, which in turn creates higher demand for goods. This results in growth in economic activity. At some point the supply cannot meet that demand and prices rise.

The increase in prices, in turn, results in higher inflation. When that inflation reaches that country's inflation target, the State Bank (or Reserve Bank) will increase interest rates to dampen demand for goods.

The cycle starts all over again, with company debt rising, so companies lay off staff and so on.

Meanwhile, all you need to know now is that demand and supply for shares reflects the public's sentiment toward a particular company, different sectors, and thus the market as a whole. In this manner the stock market is thus a leading indicator of the overall economy, by about 9 to 12 months.

In addition to owning part of a company via a shareholding, owning shares also allows you to utilize the power of compounding to earn a return on top of returns. Compounding is part of the reason that for decades stocks have outperformed practically every other investment tool.

A question I've been asked in the past is why would a company want to issue shares? Why share the profits with thousands of people when they could keep profits to themselves? The reason companies issue shares— aside from needing money (called equity financing) for expansion, upgrading equipment, or marketing—is that raising money through debt financing (bonds or credit) is simply more expensive. Effectively, equity is more popular for raising money, as there are no interest payments like there are from taking on debt.

Another benefit, as part owner of a company, is that the investor is able to vote in the running of the company. This means that he or she can attend meetings, ask questions, and get to know the company better, enabling him to make a more informed decision on the future prospects of the company.

## Other Roles of Stock Exchanges

Stock exchanges have more than just one role in the economy. In addition to funding businesses and providing individuals with a direct investment opportunity, these may include the following.

### Venture Capital and Associated Higher Risk

Listed venture firms obtain funds from the public and use these funds to invest in higher risk or start-up firms. While there are such firms on all exchanges, you find that the cost of using such firms is expensive as they tend to take a large portion of equity for providing funds.

### Research and Development Funding

Over the years, some companies raised significant capital to conduct research for the more complex industries, such as defense force, astrophysics, and chemical industries. Note that numerous tax laws have been changed to remove or limit the level at which tax can be deducted.

So, remember that you are an investor or trader and your interest is return on investment and not whether a company has a research division, unless that division is a strong profit generator.

### Finding Big Brother

Yet another source of raising capital for a private company is to find a corporate partner by offering shares in your listed company in return for assistance in marketing, sales, and diversification into new areas.

Corporate partnerships have been extremely effective in many cases.

### Create Your Own Pension

When people draw their savings and buy shares, they promote business activity.

This directs (and in certain cases, redirects) flow of funds and thus promotes specific economic sectors such as agriculture and commerce, which results in improved economic growth and higher productivity levels.

### Growth via Acquisition

Listed companies sometimes use rights issues (issuing more shares) to acquire competitors, or as an opportunity to expand product lines or divisions, or hedge against volatility.

A takeover bid or a merger agreement through the stock market is effective and relatively simple and today is quiet common. As a trader, you have to decide whether the additional profits will more than offset the added shares. For instance, if a company's attributable profit is $1,000 and the company has 1,000 shares in issue, then the EPS (Earnings per share is calculated by dividing the company's attributable profits by the companies' ordinary share in issue) will be one dollar.

If the company's PE ratio is 10 times, then the company has a share price of $10.

So, if the company issues an additional 1,000 shares to buy a competitor with profits of $500, is this a profitable share acquisition? A Price: Earnings Ratio is used for valuing a company by measuring its current share price relative to its EPS.

Aside from potential future growth, here is the current value of the share:

- Shares in issue rise to 2,000 shares.
- The net profit (ignoring restructuring costs) will be $1,500.
- The EPS is now $0.75.
- The share price on a 10 PE is now $7.50.

As a trader, would you make a profit in this investment opportunity?

### Share Incentive Schemes

The listing of a company enables entrepreneurs to retain key staff members and hire and appoint additional professional managers, thus improving managerial standards, efficiency, and productivity. They do this by offering directors and key staff members' shares in the company. Consequently, it can be stated that listed companies have better management records than privately held companies.

**Chapter 2 outlines who owns the major world exchanges.**

# CHAPTER 2

# The Stock Exchange Club

*Trading is likened to sword fighting—you have to be quick or you're dead.*

| | Exchange | Symbol | Market Cap U.S.$-trillion |
|---|---|---|---|
| 1 | New York Stock Exchange | NYSE | 18.17 |
| 2 | NASDAQ Stock Exchange | NASDAQ | 7.05 |
| 3 | Tokyo Stock Exchange | JPX | 4.6 |
| 4 | Shanghai Stock Exchange | SSE | 3.93 |
| 5 | London Stock Exchange | LSE | 3.64 |
| 6 | Euronext Amsterdam Stock Exchange | Euronext | 3.35 |
| 7 | Shenzhen Stock Exchange | SZSE | 3.09 |
| 8 | Hong Kong Stock Exchange | HKEX | 3.02 |
| 9 | Toronto Stock Exchange | TSX | 1.77 |
| 10 | German Stock Exchange | FSX | 1.66 |
| 11 | Bombay (Mumbai) Stock Exchange | BSE | 1.43 |
| 12 | Swiss Stock Exchange | SIX | 1.42 |
| 13 | India National Stock Exchange | NSE | 1.41 |
| 14 | South Korea Stock Exchange | KRX | 1.28 |
| 15 | Stockholm Stock Exchange | OMX | 1.26 |
| 16 | Australia Stock Exchange | ASX | 1.2 |
| Total | | | 58.27 |

There are 60 major stock exchanges spread throughout in the world, with the largest being the United States-based New York Stock Exchange (NYSE), which has a market capitalization of $18.5 trillion. This equates to a third of the world's listed companies.

# Club Members

Out of the 60 exchanges, only 16 exchanges form part of what has been called the "Trillion Dollar Club." This group makes up 87 percent of the world's total value of equities and adds up to $59 trillion.

# Who Dominates?

From a geographical perspective, North America and Europe control 60 percent of the world's markets, while Asia's 33.3 percent control comes from Shenzhen, Hong Kong, Tokyo, and Shanghai.

The southern hemisphere is dominated by exchanges in Australian, Indonesia, Johannesburg, and Brazil.

### Typical Structures

There are two types of securities exchanges:

- **Call Markets:** This market limits a stock to trade at only specific times and at one price. This type of market is more popular in smaller exchanges.
- **Continuous Markets:** This is the normal type of exchange, where buyers and sellers are matched up based on price and volume.

# Structural Differences

### National Stock Exchanges

These offer various forms of securities, including futures, forex, options, and bonds, driven by price and normally has stringent qualifications to be listed.

- The New York Stock Exchange (NYSE) and the American Stock Exchange (AMEX) are U.S. national stock exchanges.
- The London Stock Exchange (LSE) is the UK's national exchange.

## Regional Exchanges

- A regional exchange is characterized by smaller markets and traded.
- An example of a regional exchange is the Boston Exchange, which does not meet the listing requirements of a national exchange.

## Over-the-Counter Markets (OTC)

- This is a less formal exchange, which hosts listed and unlisted stocks and is an order-driven market, where buyers and sellers submit bids and a dealer trades from his portfolio, that is the OTC market is often referred to as a negotiated market.
- In the United States, NASDAQ is used as the quotation system for the OTC market.

## Some Exchange Listing Requirements

Listing schedules or requirements are effectively a set of conditions that companies must meet before they can become publically listed on an exchange. These conditions include profitability, years in operation, number of shares to be issued, and capitalization.

Therefore, companies must meet an exchange's requirements to have their stocks and shares listed and traded there, but requirements vary by stock exchange:

| Stock Exchange | Issued Shares | Market Cap | Earnings | Years in Operation |
|---|---|---|---|---|
| New York | 1 million | +$100 million | +$10 million | 3 |
| NASDAQ | 1.25 million | +$70 million | +$11 million | 3 |
| London | 25% of issued shares | +£700,000 | 12 months working capital | 3 |
| Bombay Stock | Equivalent to 100 million | + 250 million | Na | Na |

## Who Owns Global Exchanges?

In the past decade stock exchanges around the world have started to unbundle, which means that the members of exchanges started to sell their shares and these exchanges in turn became a listed company.

In this way the shares are listed on a stock exchange.

## Other Types of Exchanges

These include exchanges to trade forward contracts on commodities, also called future contracts. Today, these exchanges also offer future contracts on interest rates, shares, and options.

These are today commonly known as futures exchanges.

## Benefits of Exchanges

If the stock market is, indeed, the engine room of the economy, the investor can actually predict how the economy will behave in future. Or can he? Let's look at this logically.

First, companies from across the entire spectrum of industry and commerce gather at the exchange to raise capital from the public. This allows them to expand, which—in turn—promotes new jobs, products, services, and business opportunities. As profits improve, dividends are paid out to investors, who often use these to buy shares in other listed companies and, thus, the cycle of economic prosperity continues to expand.

This theory would work well if the markets continued to move on fundamentals only. What happens if the economy looks healthy, has strong growth potential, but the stock market corrects strongly. Does this mean that in 10 months' time the economy will take a nosedive? Not so!

In 1990, as a young junior analyst I was told: "We don't just analyze companies—we analyze the factors that affect shares." In other words, market sentiment plays a crucial role. So, assuming the economy is healthy and the market falls on some negative political comment or perceived threat—what does the portfolio manager do?

Well, that is really up to you. Needless to say, always look at the fundamentals of a particular stock. If the stock is all that you believe it is, then sentiment is just that—sentiment. The share often bounces back quickly and market volatility provides the trader with a market opportunity to buy.

Conversely, if market sentiment pushes a share price beyond its true value, the share will be expected to fall back within a short period of time. This provides investors with a sell opportunity.

## Comment

At the stock exchange, share prices rise and fall depending, largely, on economic forces. Share prices tend to rise or remain stable when companies and the economy in general show signs of stability and growth.

An economic recession, depression, or financial crisis could eventually lead to a stock market correction. Therefore, the movement of share prices and in general of the stock indexes can be an indicator of the general trend in the economy.

**Chapter 3 sets out ownership of the stockbroking firm and how it functions.**

# CHAPTER 3

# The Stockbroking Firm

*Take time to get to know yourself, so that you can better handle your stress level.*

## A Brief Overview of the Stockbroking Firm

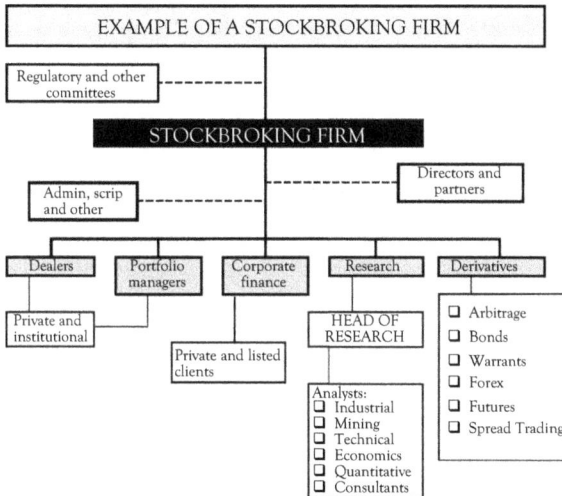

```
              EXAMPLE OF A STOCKBROKING FIRM

Regulatory and other
   committees ------------------

              STOCKBROKING FIRM
                                        Directors and
                                          partners
 Admin, scrip  ------------
 and other

 Dealers   Portfolio   Corporate   Research    Derivatives
           managers    finance
                                    HEAD OF     ❑ Arbitrage
Private and                         RESEARCH    ❑ Bonds
institutional                                   ❑ Warrants
              Private and listed                ❑ Forex
              clients                           ❑ Futures
                                    Analysts:   ❑ Spread Trading
                                    ❑ Industrial
                                    ❑ Mining
                                    ❑ Technical
                                    ❑ Economics
                                    ❑ Quantitative
                                    ❑ Consultants
```

Here is a brief breakdown of the types of people or departments that make up a stockbroking firm. I am about to disappoint many novice traders: There is, actually, no mystery to what a stock exchange is or how it operates.

The mystery and confusion about stockbrokers starts with understanding the differences between the various positions within a stockbroking firm. Often, when an investor calls to open up a trading account, he or she will ask for the stockbroker and not the dealer. Analysts are asked if they trade daily, or whether portfolio managers research duties take them out of town. Corporate financers get confused with researchers and on numerous occasions entrepreneurs will ask for traders when they actually need to speak to corporate advisors to list their companies.

If you want to be a stockbroker, which avenue do you want to pursue?

There are many different career paths and opportunities available through stock exchanges, but the aim of these three volumes are to assist individuals to trade for themselves. Therefore, while it is important to understand what makes up a stock exchange and a broking firm, the main focus is to assist you to set up a trading desk and to provide information on how to buy and sell securities.

Let's start with a description of how an exchange operates and highlight the different types of investment opportunities available to the public, their benefits and how to invest in these instruments.

There is an invisible "Chinese Wall" between these departments in an attempt to prevent insider trading from taking place. After all, if a corporate financier were to tell a dealer that Company XYZ was about to acquire a competitor, this privileged information could be used to the benefit of a few people, but to the detriment of many.

The subject of these divisions is amply covered in many financial books, so the aim in this chapter is to provide important information to understand the basics of how an exchange operates. You need this basic information to build up a foundation of knowledge before you set up your own trading desk.

Definitions of each of the following terms are provided in the glossary, so the following text concentrates on providing you with a better understanding of how each department interrelates within a stockbroking firm.

## The Stockbroker

The stockbroker forms an integral part of the free market system. He or she is the person who administers a mechanism that allows the public to acquire part ownership in companies and therefore have an indirect say in economic development.

Depending on the exchange and country you are trading in, a stockbroker can be known as a registered representative, a broker, or investment advisor. He or she is effectively a professional who executes buy and sell orders for stocks and other securities through a stock market for a stipulated fee, often on a sliding scale.

The stockbroker is thus the person who has obtained the right to be a "share administrator" by passing all relevant stock exchange examinations and all necessary registration requirements. So, when a prospective client telephones an established broker and tells the receptionist that he or she wants to buy shares, it is unlikely that the client's call will be transferred to the stockbroker. It would be more prevalent for the client to ask for his portfolio manager or for the call to be transferred to a dealer, where the deal would be carried out.

In the case of a one-man operation, the stockbroker will personally do all these tasks, but most brokers have different staff members to carry out such duties.

It must be noted that the term stockbroker today tends to refer to retail brokers. This is a stockbroking firm which deals in securities. The professional who lists companies on the exchange is called a sponsor. This term may be different depending on the exchange being used to list a business. For instance, if you wish to list a business on an SME market in South Africa (The Alternative Exchange), the broker would be called a designated advisor, while listing on the similar market in the UK (The Alternative Investment Market), you would use a nomad.

Other departments within a stockbroking firm include professionals to analyze company trends and forecast future results, maintaining portfolios, trading equities, bonds, and warrants for private or institutional clients.

### The Securities Analyst

This is a skilled person who undertakes the task of analyzing markets, trends, sectors, and companies. He or she is responsible for determining current and new market trends and forecasting future company performance, to enable him to forecast a potential share price movement.

The research division usually consists of a head of research, industrial (split into consumer and nonconsumer goods analysts), mining and technical analysts, and an economist. Some broking firms also have political analysts and quantitative and technical analysts.

Industrial analysts look at different sectors of the market and the larger stockbroking firms would have experts to analyze specific sectors, such as consumer-based goods. In turn, mining analysts are divided into their spheres of expertise, such as gold, platinum, or diamonds.

Since the mid-1980s it has become more acceptable for stockbroking firms to hire consultants to do certain tasks. The political analyst usually falls into this category.

The importance of the political analyst includes better understanding of how the potential of serious strike action could affect companies in the near future, whether it will continue or escalate, whether wage demands will rise unabated or whether trade unions will accept alternative to wage increases, for example, share incentive schemes.

In recent years, political analysts have been tasked with assessing the influence of political stability of a country on an exchange and thus on investor sentiment.

### Portfolio Managers

Clients' shares are maintained by the portfolio manager. He or she is responsible for buying and selling shares for specific clients (either private or institutional) and has to keep these clients informed on all trades carried out.

However, many of the larger institutions and brokers have executive meeting to determine what shares should be bought and often clients are placed into stocks or types of stocks that they have no control over. These three volumes set out the mechanics of portfolio management and the techniques that you can use to set up and maintain your own specific criteria for investing.

Interestingly, the required qualifications to be an analyst vary quiet radically around the world. There is an increasing trend to only employ analysts who have graduated with a master's degree in finance or has obtained the Chartered Financial Analyst (CFA) designation.

In the United States, Wall Street research analysts must also register with the Financial Industry Regulatory Authority, pass the General Securities Representative Exam and also pass the Research Analyst Examination in order to publish research on listed companies.

## Dealers and Traders

There are various types of dealers, namely private, institutional and "for own book" dealer. The latter means dealing on behalf of the stockbroking firm you are working for and not for clients. The main task of the dealer is to carry out the function trading shares on behalf of clients.

In essence, he or she carries out buy or sell orders. The difference between the private and institutional dealer is found in the type of client he or she trades shares for. In the former, the dealer trades on request from the public, while the latter deals with institutional clients, such as pension funds.

To become a dealer one starts out as an unauthorized clerk, carrying out messages, answering telephone calls, and other menial tasks. After a period of some months, the clerk is called up in front of a committee to answer questions on trading procedures. If the clerk passes this test he or she becomes an authorized clerk and his or her responsibilities are increased. He or she is thereafter able to conduct trades on behalf of clients.

## The Corporate Finance Team

The main function of corporate finance is to carry out any corporate task that involves listed companies and, in many countries today, also private companies. This includes listing or delisting a company, changing a company's name, issuing new shares, debentures, takeovers, restructuring firms, and so on.

The corporate finance department usually consists of chartered accountants or corporate lawyers, who have also passed the exchange examinations and are, thus also registered members of the exchange.

## Administration Departments

All trades are registered daily and the client will either be sent a check for shares sold or an account for shares bought.

This department is important in that it keeps a check on commission received for all trades completed.

## Arbitrage

Arbitrage is effectively buying and selling of securities at the same time. This is usually a commodities (but can also be currencies) and traded in different markets to take advantage of price discrepancies.

This term actually refers to a process rather than a department. For instance, when an exchange closes down for the night, not all traders close shop for the day. Some stockbrokers have skeleton crews working until midnight, watching the overseas exchanges, and trading in those securities.

This type of trade adds another dimension to making deals, in that the dealer can now take advantage of price discrepancy caused by currency exchange rates. This is the meaning of arbitrage.

Price discrepancies, or arbitrage, are not limited between equities across borders, but can also occur between futures markets.

## Derivatives

This "other" market was neglected and ignored by the general public for many years. It seemed too complicated and interest was usually centered in the equities market. However, to achieve a true cross-diversification of a portfolio it is essential in the long term for the investor to consider all available markets.

## Analytical Interaction of Departments

Each department has a specific use and, whether or not it provides the stockbroker with a direct income, they do help to complete the investment service offered to clients.

For instance, every morning many stockbroking firms hold a meeting that includes corporate finance, dealers, analysts, directors, and portfolio managers. The meeting is usually chaired by the economist, who outlines the latest market movements; including changes in commodities, interest rates, and currencies.

He or she explains the meaning and possible future consequence of such movements. In addition, he or she discusses any economic statistic released—GDP, consumer price index (CPI), producer price index (PPI), unemployment rates, and so on—and explains possible consequences of the figures.

This is followed by a breakdown of stock market indexes, such as the Overall, Financial, Industrial, and All Gold and Platinum indexes. It is then the analysts turn to discuss company performances (annual reports released in the press). The analyst responsible for a particular company would explain and outline future movements in the company's performance and how these would affect the share price.

The analyst would conclude by providing a recommendation on whether to buy, sell, or hold the share.

Dealers would outline the previous day's trade and, thus, market sentiment and new trends are revealed. If corporate finance needs to explain effects of changes in tax laws and so on, they would do this during the meeting.

Armed with the preceding information, dealers and portfolio managers would be able to make better-informed decisions when buying or selling shares for clients. Analysts would be able to streamline forecasts and directors would be able to know what is happening within the firm and in the market.

**As a consequence, this volume uses the structure of the stockbroking firm to enable you to set up your own trading desk, with techniques to analyze shares, and methods to build up a portfolio that is sound and one that has long-term upward potential.**

**Chapter 4 is the start of analysis, outlining different types of shares.**

# CHAPTER 4

# Investments and Shareholders

*Discipline is always the difference between winners and losers.*

## Types of Shares

Shares are sometimes referred to as stocks, securities, or equity.

There are two main types of stocks: ordinary shares (also called common stock) and preference shares.

### Ordinary Shares (Voting)

The global norm is for companies to issue ordinary shares, which are the main types of stocks traded in the market. These represent ownership in a company in the proportion of shares held. In addition to capital growth investors also receive a portion of profits in the form of a dividend. Some countries require that financials are declared every quarter, while some have two sets of financial releases a year.

As part owner of the company, shareholders have the right to vote (one vote per share) to elect the board of directors at the company's Annual General Meeting (AGM). Should a company go bankrupt and liquidate, the common shareholder will receive money only after creditors, bondholders, and preference shareholders.

### Preference Shares

**Preference shares** usually do not have voting rights, but are guaranteed a dividend before ordinary shareholders.

These take the form of:

- **Cumulative:** This carries the obligation to pay these shareholders any interest arrears resulting from years of poor trading.
- **Convertible:** This means that the shares will be converted either into debt or ordinary shares at a predetermined date.
- **A combination of the previous points.**

### Debentures

Depending on the country defining a debenture, the meaning can be completely different. In many countries in emerging markets, debentures are defined as fixed-interest securities, which are repayable to the investor at a given date and are linked to a specific assets, thus these have a high degree of security. The disadvantage of this security is a lower interest rate and does not provide ownership status.

In other countries, a debenture is a debt instrument that is not secured by physical assets. In these countries, debentures are backed by the creditworthiness of the issuer.

In the aforementioned countries, these debentures will be denoted as "unsecured."

### Rights Issue and Nil Paid Letters

After a company has been listed, it may have an opportunity to acquire one of its key competitors or to expand locally or across borders. When this occurs the company directors can decide to go back to the market for additional funding. If the directors decide to obtain additional funds from another issue of share and not from bank loans, they can offer shares from the company's "authorized" shares. They have to make an offer of new shares to existing shareholders. These new shares belong to the company itself and are not issued from the directors' personal shares.

This is called a "rights issue."

This is carried out by offering their exciting shareholders the opportunity to buy some more shares in the amount that they already own.

This way, major shareholders avoid their shareholding from being diminished. To execute this right, companies issue existing shareholders with "renounceable nil paid letters of allocation."

Known as NPLs, they entitle these shareholders the right to buy one additional share for every share they own on a specific date, called the "take-up date."

If a holder of NPLs does not take up the shares by this date, then the offer falls away and the NPLs have no further value. However, under such conditions, the shareholder has the right to sell these NPLs in the open market; already listed next to the company's listed code. In this manner, new shareholders enter the market.

## Some Investment Alternatives

The following are some of the more popular investment alternatives.

### Fixed Interest and Other Bank Deposits

While bank deposits et al. have a place in the market, these are not investment opportunities.

Every trader should have at least 6 months' worth of salary in a bank account, which should at least earn interest close to the inflation rate. Therefore, this is more of a short-term saving tool to meet a specific need, rather than an effort to achieve profit.

Therefore, while having a strong cash holding does not provide a trader with a real return, it does provide much needed stability for his daily trading activities.

### Fixed Property

Large sums of cash are tied up for considerable periods of time. There is no doubt that over the past two decades property investors have made significant returns, but remember that such fixed assets usually require future additional capital outlays to maintain or improve the value of the property.

There are two additional issues that must be remembered:

- Fixed property cannot be easily sold and takes time for legal requirements to be met, including municipal, provincial, and state taxes and other expenses.
- There are transfer costs and capital gains taxes to be taken into account.

Remember that property shares can always form a part of a portfolio of shares, which can be sold quickly when the property market turns; certainly quicker than trying to sell the actual property.

### Entrepreneurial Endeavors

This risk of buying shares in an unlisted company is the lack or difficulty in an exit strategy.

This method is only desirable for investors who are prepared to wait indefinitely to recoup their investment. Large capital outlays are usually needed and often exclude the small investor.

### The Bond (Gilt) Market

Also called gilts, bonds offer traders an alternative investment options. Note that these do not offer part ownership in companies or other organizations.

These tend to be issued by the state (i.e., parastatals and local municipalities), utilities (electricity companies, water providers, etc.), or companies.

Bonds are offered at a discount and pay a fixed rate of interest with a low associated risk. For instance, if a 5-year bond costs $1 million, has a 10 percent discount rate , and an annual interest of 15 percent, then a trader:

- Would buy the bond at $900,000.
- Earn an interest of 15 percent a year; often payable every 6 months.
- Receive $1 million back from the issuer in 5 years' time.

Although the nominal value of bonds remains constant, supply and demand influences prices.

While it may be expensive to buy bonds, the astute investor and trader would use bonds as a contra-cyclical strategy to equities. The alternative is to acquire a cheaper bond option or futures contract. Of course, bonds are also traded on the exchange.

The reason bonds are issued is to obtain funds to meet long-term financial commitments such as building roads, hospitals, providing electricity, or paying for large-scale mergers. The larger institutions, including insurance, mutual funds, and financial services companies, are the main purchasers of bonds.

### Warrants (Also called Options)

A warrant is best explained as buying a claim on a share for its future value. These are divided into "call" and "put" warrants. The former is a claim that a share will rise and the latter a claim that the share will fall.

There are three main reasons for buying warrants.

- First, to generate income, which is achieved as sellers of warrants demand a premium on these instruments sold.
- Second, and often the reason for buying the warrant— there is a speculative aspect that is very attractive to traders. A London stockbroker once described warrants as "appealing to investors with a speculative urge, but who insisted on having a specially designed safety net." If buyers and sellers accurately judge future movement in the overall stock exchange index, they can substantially increase their profits.
- Finally, an investor can use a warrant to protect his personal portfolio against adverse market movements. For instance, if he or she believes that the overall market prices will fall in 3 months, he or she can take out a put warrant and, therefore, protect his or her investment. In addition, an investor can mix bonds and warrants.

An old colleague at the JSE, in early 2015, advised me to buy "put gilt warrants." This means that he believed that the bonds market would be in a bull run within 6 months and that for every 100th of a percent that the gilt fell, I would earn R500. A mental calculation revealed that the gilt had to rise by only 200th of a percent for my investment to breakeven.

By the time I wanted to take up the warrant, it was too late. The gilt bull was in its zenith and the investment viability was lost.

The opportunity cost of not taking the risk of the venture became hypothetical and a hard lesson to learn. There are more ways of investing in the stock market than through the equity market. Take cognizance of all available securities, how you can benefit from them, take advantage of cross diversification, and open your mind to new methods.

In many instance, where novice traders need to learn the lesson of patience and focus, mentors will advise clients to buy warrants. The aim is to show such traders that warrants—at some point—will expire; fall to zero. As such, it is an important way to teach clients the ability to compare risk to reward as they have to continuously value their investment by looking at:

- Strike price
- Current price
- Conversion ratio
- Potential ultimate earnings

Let's assess the preceding list.

- Warrant X costs 100 cents.
- The basis is 6 months and paired to Stock A, which is trading at 95 cents.
- The split is 10:1 (called *the contract*).
- Strike price 105 cents.

This means that, if your analysis determines that, Stock A's share price will rise (e.g., 120 cents) within 6 months before the warrant's expiry date, then you would buy Warrant X to take advantage of the conversion rate of one warrant contract for 10 Stock A at the price of 105 cents.

The calculation would be to multiply Stock A's share by the number of contracts you have taken, for instance if you bought 10 Warrants X, you would have bought 10 contracts. Then subtract the cost of the warrant and the decision would be yours to take up the conversion or not.

You could also trade the warrant as the price moves in the market. Note that you would only be "In the Money" once the share has moved past the strike price.

### Share Installments

Share installments are effectively loans to buy shares.

They enable traders to optimize his or her exposure to the share market by making only a partial payment for their shares. For a portion of their current price, they get the benefit of ownership in the form of capital growth and dividends.

So, when you buy a share installment, you initially pay only a portion of the current share price, but the buyer is entitled to the same benefits that he or she or would enjoy had they bought the entire share.

By paying less upfront, you increase your share exposure by the gearing offered. If you want, you can pay the balance of the share price (i.e., the loan amount) at any time before the share installment matures, but this is not compulsory. If the share price falls you will not be subject to margin calls and you will not be required to repay the loan. As share installments are listed on some global exchanges, they are highly liquid.

Interestingly, share installments have some benefits over shares, namely:

- **Faster wealth creation:** You have the opportunity to earn profits and dividends from a larger investment portfolio than you would normally be able to hold.
- **No margin calls:** As repayment of the loan is optional, you are not committed to further payments if the value of your share installment drops.
- **Listing:** These instruments can be bought and sold like ordinary shares.

## The Futures Market

Despite being one of the most potentially profitable markets available to traders, it remains a highly misunderstood one. Analysts are unsure why these markets have not gained popularity in many emerging markets, but they guess reasons lie in understanding the complexities of new instruments. Although futures in the United States is mostly linked to actual commodities, such as orange juice, pork bellies or wheat, the trend is to link these to financial markets.

For instance, an investor could buy a futures contract—bull or bear—on the Petroleum Index. If he or she believes that the index will fall in the next 3 months, he or she can acquire a bear futures contract which will enable him or her to make money, despite a fall in the price of petroleum. In such an instance the investor has not bought actual petrol, but has bought the risk of movement in the price of that commodity. The greatest advantage of the futures market lies in the ability of investors to hedge and thus protect their investments against future market risks.

## Spread Trading

Also known as *Contracts for Difference* (CFD) trading in the institutional marketplace, it is an alternative to traditional trading in equities. With spread trading you never take ownership of any stock. All you are buying is the price movement in the stock, or bond, currency or commodity.

One benefit of spread trading is that you can make money whether markets are rising or falling. You can buy a CFD on a security or index if you believe that it will a rise in price (called, going long) or you can buy if you believe the security or index will fall in value (called, going short).

One of the primary attractions of spread trading is gearing, which means that you have the potential to earn large profits on small movements in the underlying share, bond, index, commodity, or currency. Spread trading gearing levels range from about 6 times on individual stocks to 50 times on bonds and currencies.

You nominate the risk you're prepared to take. For example, more conservative investors can nominate one dollar per point move the UK's FTSE 100 index. More aggressive investors can increase this to $25 or even $50 per point.

In October 2015 I recommended that investors buy a CFD on Company X, which had announced that it was unbundling a division by separately listing that division, called Company Y. The forecast was that Company Y would list at $20 a share, which would reduce the share price of Company X to $80 a share. The analysis suggested that Company X share price would rise by at least $10 over a 3-month period.

With gearing, a $5,000 investment in a CFD equaled to $8 point movement for every 1 cent Company X share price moved. In the 5 days after the listing of Company Y, the share price rose by $6, which equaled to a profit of $4,800 on an investment of $5,000 (600 cents movement × $8 percent movement).

Stated differently, in 5 days investors made a 96 percent return on their $5,000 investment.

### Unit Trusts

The aim of unit trusts is twofold:

- To protect the investors' capital against inflation
- Capital growth

Compared to investing in shares, the risk is lower, but should be considered as long term. The objective is to pay for a specialist to buy and manage a spread of shares for you. Although unit trusts usually provide real returns, they are a composition of blue chip shares and, therefore, often only reflect current stock market trends.

### Gold Coins

The most popular gold coin is the Kruger Rand for South Africa, which is 22 carat bullion, weighing one troy ounce. It is considered a safe haven against bear trends in equities markets.

### Other Less Liquid Markets

These include Persian carpets, coin or stamp collecting, antiques, and paintings. The investor relies on his or her knowledge of the item and its future potential value. The primary issue in making such investments depends on the investor's knowledge or perception of the future value of new artworks.

The risk is great and often far exceeds the return. In addition, these have to be ensured at great expense.

## Shareholders' Rights

When you buy shares, a central securities depositary will record your name and various other personal details in an electronic register proving ownership of the shares. Once you own shares in a company, you have certain important rights, including:

- **Attend AGMs:** You are entitled to attend and vote at the meetings of the shareholders of the company. Companies are required to hold an Annual General Meeting (AGM) at which the directors report back to the shareholders on the progress which has been made during the year. Important decisions affecting the future of the company are made at this meeting by a simple majority vote. Each ordinary share of the company entitles the holder to one vote. The company can also call a special meeting during the year to decide on a specific issue.
- **Dividends:** You are entitled to receive your share of the dividend of the company. Each year the directors look at the profits made by the company and decide how much to pay out as a dividend. Usually, they will keep some of the profits in the company to plough back for future growth. This money is known as "retained earnings."
- **Financial statements:** You are entitled to receive the annual financial statements of the company. Different countries may have slightly different rules, but under *International Financial Reporting Standards* (IFR Standards) a single set of accounting standards has been developed and maintained by the International Accounting Standards Board (the Board). The aim is to standardize accounting practices in developed and emerging economies.

a. IFR Standards are supported by more than 100 countries, including the European Union and by more than 66 percent of the G20.

- **Liquidation:** If the company is liquidated, you are entitled to receive your share of the remaining assets of the company once the creditors have all been paid. If the controlling shareholders are made an offer for their shares, then you are entitled to be made the same offer for your shares.

**Part 2, Chapter 5 explains Wall Street Rules to better trading techniques.**

# PART II
# Trading Rules for Beginners

# CHAPTER 5

# Wall Street's Golden Rules

*Discipline, knowledge, and experience are the pillars to trading success.*

Wall Street is looked at by many as the global guru of all that is financial. And, indeed, over the decades many practical rules of thumb have surfaced. These axioms, as some call them, are based on years of accumulated experience and trial-and-error results. The simple truth is that these axioms do have merit and should be outlined in a book on trading and as such should be incorporated in your personal trading rules.

So, some of the more important Wall Street axioms have been especially selected for this volume. However, I prefer to start with golden rules of Wall Street that are interesting and certainly can be used as part of your rules.

## The Nine Essential Golden Rules

### Golden Rule 1: Never Buy

*Never buy a share that won't rise in a bull market.*

If traders who have extensive knowledge of the market start selling shares, should you follow or should you buy? For whatever reason, these traders are not buying that stock, so there surely must be a reason, which may not be apparent, but it exists anyway.

### Golden Rule 2: Shorting Bears

*Never sell a stock short that won't decrease in a bear market.*

Those traders "in the know"—let's call them Insiders—are selling a stock—should you not follow?

### Golden Rule 3: Shorting Bulls

*Sell a stock short that won't increase in a bull market the moment the market turns bearish.*

A stock that can't attract buying support when everything else is moving ahead must have something radically wrong with it. Therefore, the stock would be vulnerable in a bear trend.

### Golden Rule 4: Bears

*Buy a stock that won't decrease in a bear market.*

It is believed that these shares will lead the next market upswing. This is in my opinion one of the most effective rules on Wall Street. It simply suggests that a share that is supported by the masses is so strong that new buying will push it up when bulls return to the market.

### Golden Rule 5: Sympathy Stocks

*Don't buy the "sympathy" stock. It is seldom profitable.*

If XYZ Widget Corp's share is rising, but ABC Widget's is not, don't buy ABC just because it has a similar name. Stocks do tend to move in industry groups, but something may be happening at XYZ that has no bearing on ABC.

### Golden Rule 6: Bulls to Bears

*When a bull market turns to bear, sell the stock that has risen the most.*

The technical traders suggest that stock which have risen the most have created the largest gap in the market. Therefore, these stocks should react the most to a downswing. This may seem to be a contradiction, but it isn't. Actually, stocks that have had the greatest percentage rise frequently have created the largest gap between fair value and current price, so also have a great percentage potential correction or downswing.

### Golden Rule 7: Increasing Stocks

*Sell the stock that has increased the least.*

Shares that falter and do not increase in price, eventually fall. This is in agreement with Rule No. 3. If the stock can't attract buyers, it often attracts sellers, as traders and investors buy shares for an expected capital growth. A share that isn't moving is an opportunity cost.

### Golden Rule 8: Bears to Bulls

*When a bear market turns to bull, buy the stock that has decreased the most, and also the stock that has decreased the least.*

These two principles are not contradictory. Instead, they illustrate two extremes, showing the greatest percentage declines are normally due for percentage previous gains. Stocks that have held up best have a reason for doing so, hence, are in a position to attract new support.

### Golden Rule 9: Take Immediate Action

*If a stock is a purchase or a sale, action should be taken at once.*

The market does not consider your trade in its fluctuations. In other words, if buying or selling is imperative, action should be taken at once. Such transactions should be made immediately at the price offered by the market.

## Wall Street Axioms

### Axiom 1: Vigilance

*Eternal vigilance is the price of safety.*

Successful traders in the past believed that they should watch the market constantly and religiously. Above all, they emphasized the sense of timing. As Jay Gould, the famous U.S. speculator put it: "The perfect speculator must know when to come in; more important, he must know when to stay out; and most important, he must know when to get out once he is in!"

### Axiom 2: Speculation and Investments

*A good investment is a good speculation, but if it is not a good speculation, it is not even a safe investment.*

While speculation has its place in markets, there should always be an element of analysis, whether fundamental or technical. Anything else is pure guesswork.

### Axiom 3: Taking Profits

*No man ever makes himself poor by taking profits.*

This was a favorite axiom of old Commodore Vanderbilt. It certainly paid off handsomely in his experience. The Commodore was fond of remarking that "paper profits can quickly turn into losses, unless carefully supervised and acted on."

### Axiom 4: Minds of Men

*The market is made by the minds of men. What the minds of men have made, your mind can solve.*

As constantly emphasized, the psychological factor in trading is critical. Stocks sell on the basis of what investors think at a given time. Above all, try to sense, to evaluate, investor psychology at all times.

### Axiom 5: Do Nothing

*If you do not see the way clear, do nothing.*

Daniel Drew, an 1880s' speculator, believed fervently in this principle. He used to say that unless the way looked clear, buying stocks in those circumstances "was like buying cows by candlelight."

### Axiom 6: Tomorrow

*The market will be here tomorrow.*

A missed opportunity is not a crisis.

Andrew Carnegie had special talents for "watching and waiting." He would calculate all his operations, whether in industry or in the stock market; but would bide his time until the "right moment." Even if you miss an opportunity today, new ones are always developing in the marketplace.

### Axiom 7: Free Resources

*Always have some resources free for bargains.*

This is one great difference between the successful and unsuccessful traders. Baron Rothschild made it an iron clad rule to keep a good part of his capital free for such bargains to be able to "buy when others are selling" … so that he could later "sell when others are buying."

### Axiom 8: Sleeping Point

*If your stocks worry you, sell to the sleeping point.*

When you can't sleep because you are worried about the value of your portfolio, it means that you are too heavily invested in selected stocks. Under such circumstances, you should "sell to the sleeping point."

This is the point where you are no longer kept awake by worrying about your shares. In other words, a practical example would be to sell enough of a share that has risen rapidly, to recoup your original cost. That way you retain the share that is rising, but have no cost associated; that is, these shares are effectively *free*.

### Axiom 9: Grist and Mills

*No grist can be ground with water that has run past the mill.*

For those who do not know what a grist is: *A corn that is ground to make flour.*

It is important to learn from investment mistakes, but as important to forget that an opportunity has been lost. They are indeed gone forever.

Instead, focus on the future and your next trade. That is a much better use of your energy.

### Axiom 10: Speculation and Certainty

*Speculation begins where certainty ends.*

All trades and investments have an element of risk. Remember the old adage: The higher the expected reward, the higher the associated risk. As you go down the scale of market cap, the element of stability and certainty reduces and risk increases proportionately.

### Axiom 11: Caution

*Caution is the father of security.*

Many experts suggest that the more careful you are, the better your chances of trading success. While it is a matter of record that most of trading losses are by careless amateurs, operating blindly and without an intelligent plan. Put differently, stick to a set of strategic variables and that will take care of decision making. In this way you are automatically careful and avoid making mistakes based on emotions.

### Axiom 12: Right and Wrong

*Nobody is always right, but successful people are more often right than wrong.*

This is a truism: even master traders make mistakes. The difference is that their overall average of making profits is higher than losses. That is the quintessence of success in the stock market; make profits most of the time.

### Axiom 13: Strikes

*Never sell stocks on account of a strike.*

The logic underlying this rule is that strikes (no matter how serious) are temporary affairs. Sooner or later, they are settled. Of course, a long strike can hurt the share price, but as a trader, look at these as opportunities to get a stock that will ultimately rise again.

### Axiom 14: Inactivity

*Do not sell a security, which has long been inactive, just as soon as it begins to move forward.*

Find the reason why a stock has been inactive. A sudden movement suggests a change in corporate activity.

### Axiom 15: Cut Losses

*Cut your losses short and let your profits run.*

This is only common sense applied to your trading.

The answer is in theory simple: Cut shares that hit your stop loss. In practice, traders panic and hope that the situation will turn and the share will bounce.

### Axiom 16: Being Reckless

*Do not plunge recklessly after one or more successful trades.*

Again, psychology enters the mind of the trader: Repeatedly making profits may give you then sense that you can do no wrong. This sense ultimately proves fatal.

### Axiom 17: Diversify

*Diversify your holdings.*

The best portfolio structure is to be invested in at least three different sectors and across the market cap spectrum.

### Axiom 18: Not Trading

> *Unless in a position to protect a trade against extreme possibilities, it is a good rule not to trade at all.*

In other words, always protect yourself with "stop-loss" orders, so as not to be caught by a sudden reversal in the market. A better stop-loss strategy is to have a training stop loss and *always* stick to that strategy. If you avoid selling a share that falls to that stop loss, you only have yourself to blame.

### Axiom 19: Bulls, Bears, and Hogs

> *Bulls win. Bears win. Hogs get slaughtered.*

I believe that this is one of the soundest rules on Wall Street. Greed has caused too many traders to fail in the market, simply because too many wait too long to buy or sell. Waiting for the right time doesn't mean waiting till the price has moved into a new trend, rather it is getting in or out before everyone else does.

### Axiom 20: Being Repetitive

> *The market seldom does the same thing more than three times in succession.*

It seldom makes the same "high" or same "low" more than three times in succession. Therefore, be constantly on the alert for "triple tops" and "triple bottoms."

### Axiom 21: Stops

> *After a long rise, place stops close to, but under the previous week's low.*

This rule is especially true in strong bull trends. Whenever a stock declined under the previous week's low, it was usually the forerunner of a sharp decline and often indicated the end of the advance. This rule was excellent "safety insurance."

### Axiom 22: Being Wrong

*Don't stay wrong long.*

Sooner or later, all traders make their share of mistakes in the market. But you can always rectify your error. If you're mistakenly bullish, turn bearish. Conversely, if you're a bear and are wrong, adjust yourself to the trend. Don't let pride, stubbornness, or prejudice blind you if you have planned wrong. Learn how to change with the tide.

### Axiom 23: Desire and Money

*The mere desire to make money should never be the mainspring for speculative actions, but only when an opportunity exists.*

This takes a great deal of discipline, but it is sound advice. No matter how much cash you have ready for investment, don't invest unless a clear opportunity exists. Opportunities are not long in developing in the market.

### Axiom 24: Price

*Buy only when the outlook warrants, price being secondary.*

Even a "low-priced" stock is not "cheap" if it won't go up. By the same token, even a "high-priced" stock is a buy if it is forecast to climb.

### Axiom 25: Timing

*The market always does what it should do, but not always when.*

Sometimes the market can be frustratingly slow in its reaction to fundamental and technical triggers. But ultimately it does return to fair value.

Patience in the sphere of trading is easier when you have a predetermined strategy.

### Axiom 26: Be Logical

> *Be bullish in a bull market; be bearish in a bear market. Do not be either a bull or a bear all the time.*

Many traders are either bulls or bears, and tend to crowbar reasons for being continuously such a trader. Ultimately, this becomes expensive until you learn to be more analytical, understanding when to go long and when to go short.

Learn to recognize the bull and bear signals and have a strategy for both.

# Myths

Time to point out and correct a few of the popular myths about share trading. There are many myths about trading, and we can't outline all in this chapter, so here are some of the more dangerous myths which to traders should be aware of. My intension is to replace these with more realistic concepts to build a foundation to knowledge.

### Myth 1: Casinos

In recent years, some of these myths have been countered by a 7-year bull run, particularly when compared to the volatility of the 1980s and 1990s. In 1994 to 1995, as columnist for the *Mail & Guardian*, I wrote about the casino comparisons many traders used when buying and selling shares. After numerous interviews, I became astutely aware that some traders saw the stock market as nothing more than an opportunity to make money from volatility. I asked a number of traders how they took advantage of the market? Their reply was at times surprising.

One trader told me that the market was there to take advantage off by moving market sentiment. "When markets are radically volatile, it is only a matter of time before we see a crash!"

We did see a market crash in 1998, but it was not restricted to any specific country. Markets around the world fell, but an interesting issue became highlighted during the subsequent rebound. The world had turned its focus on emerging markets and the future would never be the same. Globalization means that markets, whether in South Africa, China, or Brazil, are the focus of traders from around the world and cannot be totally influenced by secular sentiment.

This has been proven since 1995 by phenomenal growth in stock markets, on the back of, among other, rising oil prices, war on terrorism, the rising economic influences of Mainland China and the European Community.

In the stock market, analysts are continually forecasting future share prices by taking into account environmental influences of global and local markets. This is why stock prices fluctuate—because the outlook for business conditions are continually and rapidly changing, and consequently, so do share prices.

So, ordinary shareholders expect their returns to be volatile, but they also expect them to be positive in the long run and higher than the return on bonds, treasury bills, or other less risky investments. Despite volatility and stock market crashes, stocks have trended steadily higher in value over the years; *see appendixes.*

It is this continuous uptrend in the value of markets around the world that sets the stock market apart from gambling. In addition, if a trader is reckless in his or her purchasing of stocks, remember that the trader will still own the stock even if the share price falls. In gambling, you either win or lose.

It is thus critical that you know from the start that investing and gambling are two completely different pursuits. When you understand this, your trading strategy will become more focused and less affected by fear and greed.

### Myth 2: Why Research?

Some traders believe that, in order to be successful, you must be able to predict general stock market movement and a company's trading range. These traders say that if you can determine a company's trading range, then you can buy when it reaches the lower price range and sell when its gets to the top of the range.

And they do this by only using a set of technical indicators or triggers. Stated differently, they use buying patterns and historic trends to forecast price movements. In addition, they believe that technical analysis encompasses all factors that could influence a share price. In other words, you can ignore research or any fundamental analysis on the company, its financials or corporate deals.

There is a reason why nearly every large retail brokerage firm has a chief economist or market strategist and a team of analysts, whose main responsibilities are to predict the climate for stocks.

If results are any indication, the conclusion must be that trading without thorough research is prone to failure. One of the purposes of these three volumes is to free you from the compulsion we all seem to have to trade without a plan.

The key is to develop a plan that has a long-term focus, with a short-term safety net. Such a method would place a limit on potential losses, while riding the upward movement. This should ensure that your returns are better than general market trends.

This method looks at and concentrates on how shares are actually doing, compared to how they could do in the future.

Example:

- Share C is trading at $30.
- It reached a high of $37 in the past 12 months and a low of $33.
- According to your long-term analysis, the share could reach $45 in the next 18 months, due to a host of fundamental factors, that is, restructuring, management change, new merger, and so on.
- In the short term, however, factors (cyclical nature) could see the share fall by an unknown amount.
- To protect this investment, the independent stockbroker places a 5-percent stop loss on the share. This means that if the share falls by 5 percent, the share gets sold.
- However, to secure future (long-term) profits, the stop loss is made a "Trailing" one. This means that if the share rises to $35, the stop loss becomes $33.

This way, the trader has a plan to keep the share for 18 months, while securing his or her short-term profits. In the long run, a good investment strategy that does not rely on forecasts and analysis will fail.

## Myth 3: Stocks and Gravity

The obvious statement "what goes up must come down" may be true under the laws of gravity, but these do not rule in the world of finance and stockbroking. I have repeatedly heard traders say that a specific share has "climbed so high that it must come down."

Why? If the company has performed well and is better off financially this year when compared to last year, why would the share price come down? If the company gets bigger next year and improves sales and cost efficiencies, why should it not have a share price that is better next year than this year?

The answer lies in the influence of sentiment on company share prices. People buy and sell shares and when a share has climbed rapidly, they tend to panic and sell. Under the guise of "taking profits" traders sell. When the share hits a level that is acceptable in the minds of these traders—and in view of the future financial prospects of this company—the share tends to rise again.

The important thing to remember is that at some point, these shares advance to where they will never again return to their previous levels. As we have noted previously, stock investors demand a permanent return on their investments, just as investors in other types of assets demand a permanent return on theirs.

Some individual stocks do go up rapidly, and then give back the entire gain just as rapidly. All experienced investors and traders have had this disappointing experience. However disappointing it may be to have a good profit going and then see it evaporate, do not let this bitter experience lead you to believe in taking profits too quickly. If you do, it will cost you the really big gains, in the long run.

Of course, the grain of truth in this myth is the fact that any share trend consists of a series of advances and retreats, resulting in a net increase over time. If you are going to believe the statement "what goes up must come down," then keep in mind that it often happens that a stock moves much higher than the fall that happens during profit taking. Think of it this way: If a share increases tenfold in value and then undergoes a 20-percent correction, you are still ahead by eightfold.

Another expression is to buy good stocks when there is profit taking. Note that many of the best-performing stocks do not have significant pullbacks, while they are increasing in value. By waiting for a good stock to pull back, you will most likely doom yourself to sitting on the sidelines while a stock makes a tremendous move upward, without you. When it finally does have the pullback you've been waiting for, that could be the beginning of the stock's demise.

### Myth 4: Buy Low, Sell High

This myth is propagated by so many, from novice to top professional traders. The issue that is seldom stated is what is the low price and when has the share reached its high level?

Not knowing these basic variables leads many traders to commit major trading errors.

For instance, how do you know that a share that has fallen will not continue to fall? One of the most common investor mistakes is to buy stocks that have fallen. The issue is really to understand and be able to calculate the fair value of a share. That way, when a share falls below that fair value, then you can buy, depending on your personal set of entry levels.

If you are to succeed in the stock market, you must remove from your mind the theory that a share that has fallen offers value. It is your trading strategy that will determine whether or not you reap the benefits of the winners you find.

**Chapter 6 pinpoints mistakes and pitfalls which traders face every day.**

# CHAPTER 6

# Common Mistakes and Pitfalls

*Be wary, patient, a little cynical, determined, and rational at all times.*

There are some cautionary points to consider before you proceed to actually buying shares. The following are some common mistakes many novice traders make when entering the world of stock markets.

## Trading Mistakes

### Mistake 1: Not Doing Anything

Once you have developed a strategy to enter the market, what are you waiting for?

There is never a guarantee that the market will go up on your first day of trading, but if your strategy is fair and reasonable, then you would have entry and exit levels planned. The market may not be at your planned level to enter, but not placing a bid means that you have no confidence in your trading abilities.

As such, it is a truism that doing nothing at all will ultimately not provide you with a comfortable retirement.

A client came to me in the late 2015 and asked me what he should do with his investment in JSE-listed IT Giant Dimension Data. He had bought the shares in June 2000 when they were trading at 350 cents. The share then proceeded to climb to over R70 a share, but he kept them—refusing to sell. By 2003 the share had fallen to below 300 cents. In 2004, they underwent another recovery—this time to just under 650 cents—and still didn't sell.

Not taking active participation meant a major loss.

### Mistake 2: Starting Late

Postponing your trading aspirations is only detrimental to you. You already know that the earlier you start the better off you are.

### Mistake 3: Investing and Debt

A common mistake is to believe that you have to pay off all your debt before you start trading. This is not the case. If is like stating that you have to pay off your car before you go on holiday.

If you are prepared to be a trader, then this becomes your career. You will have credit cards and vehicles and home loans. Take these factors into account when you are planning your trading strategy.

### Mistake 4: Short-Term Investing

There is only one absolute in becoming a trader: you need at least 6 months' worth of salary in a money market account. Professionals will tell you to only use funds to invest in the stock market that you won't need for at least 3 years.

Really?

Plan and strategize. Then go for it…

### Mistake 5: Playing Safe

If you're young, most of your investing should be in the stock market. You have enough time to weather any market fluctuations and to reap the rewards of long-term gains. This doesn't mean that you cannot trade the shorter term markets, like futures.

Always remember that the better you strategy may be, the less risky your trading will ultimately be, as you gain experience and skill.

### Mistake 6: High Risk Shares

Not every trade is an opportunity and not every investment is for you.

You must determine your risk profile before you start your trading escapades. A financial mentor can help you to determine your psychological and risk-investing profile.

### Mistake 7: Trading In and Out of the Market

The serious trader *always* has a well-prepared, yet flexible, long-term plan. Flexible, in that he or she should also be prepared to take short-term profits. Essentially, you should form regular trading as part of your long-term plan.

I am not suggesting that you should trade daily, as every trade comes with brokerage fees and country-related taxes. These often reduce short-term profits to break even.

# Pitfalls

### Pitfall 1: Not Understanding

If a trader buys securities he or she do not have a fundamental understanding of the triggers that could move this company's share price, then simply put, he or she is placing each trade at risk. Trading without knowledge is pure guesswork.

### Pitfall 2: Do You Have Risk Tolerance?

If a trader is targeting higher returns, but such strategy is causing sleepless nights, he or she should shift strategy to a more conservative, lower risk mixture of stocks.

### Pitfall 3: Ignoring Trading Costs

Take account of all costs of buying *and* selling a stock. For instance, if a share costs 100 cents and costs of acquiring that share equates to 5 cents, then your acquisition costs are 105 cents. This means that the share has to rise by 5 percent before you break even.

Now, add the cost of selling the share and include taxes. Note that if you buy shares irregularly, you will be charged capital gains tax, but if you trade regularly (say, twice a week), you may be declared as a full-time trader and taxed at the full rate.

Assume that you get charged with only capital gains. You have to add this to your purchase price. This could push up the full share price to 112 cents a share. This means that you have to see the share rise by 12 percent before you break even.

Now, in terms of break even, you need to add inflation rate to achieve a real return on your investment. If the inflation rate is 5 percent, then your share must rise by an additional 5 percent.

One way to offset some of those costs is to trade through a limited company. In this way you can deduct costs associated to you company, such as office, telephonic bills, computer equipment, and Internet costs. For a more comprehensive strategy, send me a request for information to jacques@bci.za.com.

### Pitfall 4: What Is Your Exit Plan?

A plan should always have an exit strategy. A strategy could be to sell the share when it reaches a 25-percent positive growth or a 15-percent decline. The issue is simple: Always have these plans set out before out make your investment. Before you buy the share, you have no emotional attachment to it, which means you can make totally rational decisions. Once you own the stock, you tend to get either greedy or scared. These emotions lead to a desire to preserve profits, leading to prematurely cutting off an ascending price trend.

Continuous losses impact a trader's mental state, which then seems to perpetuate additional losses, breaking your trading confidence. An exit plan is thus one thing that an experienced trader always has before initiating a position. The reason is simple: You must have a plan and stick to it, or else every decision you make will be emotional, not rational.

Worse yet, some traders chase losing positions with even larger trades without proper analysis, hoping that they will quickly recover losses. Guess what? Losses escalade into critical financial fiasco. Some traders are effectively run out of their trading career.

An exit strategy must be clear cut, be completed and implemented before the trade is made. Such a strategy should cover all possible variables, outcomes, and expected returns, whether profitable or not.

### Pitfall 5: Portfolio Imbalances

A Portfolio must always be balanced. This means that you should have a relatively equal amount of funds in each share that you have in a portfolio.

This will prevent any single stock (or small group) to influence the entire portfolio.

Imagine that you have a portfolio of 10 shares, each worth about $10,000. This portfolio of $100,000 suddenly climbs to $140,000, all due to a single stock rising by 40 percent. Now, logic states that you don't sell a stock that is climbing, but you also don't want to be held at ransom by a single share.

I know that you could have a trailing stop loss to prevent significant losses if that share suddenly falls. The point is that there are times when a stop loss is bypassed. The share may have risen rapidly on the news or rumor that it is about to be acquired by a larger company. If those negotiations fail and cause the company to be declared bankrupt, the share price will fall past your stop loss. Following that, trade in this company will be suspended and ultimately terminated.

You had the option to sell the share at the higher price, but you didn't? What should you have done?

There are strategies that can be implemented, which is a combination of the aforementioned. You could, for instance, sell enough of that company's (Comp A) shares to recoup your original cost and buy another share (Comp B) that meets your portfolio strategy.

Now, do the following:

- Remove Comp A out of your active portfolio. These are effectively free shares as you recouped your original cost.
- Company B would be a share that is in the same sector as the one you sold or took out of your portfolio.
- Your main trading portfolio is back in balance.

Remember that taking too large of a position (caused a portfolio imbalance) often leads to emotional attachments that could lead to poor and ineffective trading decisions. It also exposes the trader to possible significant portfolio damage, sometimes irrevocable.

### Pitfall 6: Failure to Cut Losses

Some shares fall and do not bounce back.

Many novice traders believe that a share *must* bounce if it falls. This is a trading pitfall that sees novice traders begin to move from analysis to hope that the share falls. Every share has a level that is considered to be its fair value. If the share falls below that fair value, then it is an opportunity to see the share potentially bounce.

Such shares must be sold if they hit your stop loss.

There are times when shares that fall past fair value continue to fall. While this is a fact that should form part of a trader's strategy, their actions are often opposite any logical course of action. Many hold on to these losers, hoping against hope that the stock will consolidate and return to its upswing.

Opportunity cost is another reason to sell a share that is falling. So, beware of the emotional compulsion to hold onto falling shares.

### Pitfall 7: Selling Too Soon

Although selling a share too early might seem to be a relatively minor problem, it can actually become a serious one. In a properly diversified portfolio the potential profit from any one stock is far more than the potential loss.

That's simply another way of saying that the most you can lose on a single stock is 100 percent of what is invested, but the potential gain from every stock is unlimited. If your objective is to make as much money as you can, then you must put yourself into a position to hold onto really big winners when they come your way.

If you have a strategy that emphasizes taking the money and running every time you get a double or triple, then you are seriously limiting your portfolio.

I believe the reason most investors fail to hold onto winners long enough is that they simply do not realize how big a move can sometimes be realized. They wrongly assume that if a stock has doubled or tripled then that is about the best they can hope for.

Sometimes a stock that has doubled will go on to make another ten-fold increase. It can take years for this type of move to occur, but over a several years chances of finding a huge upward trend is far better than first imagined.

Another insidious reason for investors selling too soon is the use of price objectives. This is when you buy a stock and set a price that you will sell at if and when the stock makes it to the target price. These target prices are usually arrived at as a certain percentage above the entry price, or else are based on some analyst's assessment of the "value" of the stock.

The use of target selling prices is a seriously flawed practice. One of the enigmas of the stock market is the tendency for what seems overvalued to keep going higher still, and what seems reasonably valued or cheap to keep on retreating. The reason is that when a company's earnings are growing rapidly, the price of the stock may be high relative to the current earnings, but only a few times the following year's actual earnings.

The stock may even be selling for many times the earnings estimate for next year, because it takes time for good trends to be recognized and assimilated by stock analysts. Thus, stock analysts' earnings estimates for coming years tend to lag when something good is brewing, just as they often lag when bad things are in the works. The thing to remember about this is that the aggregate consensus of all market participants tends to be more accurate than published earnings estimates.

The use of price-selling targets mostly results in you capping your profits, as you cannot possibly make more of a profit than that which is reflected in the target price. It should also be obvious that a strategy that caps both loses and winners will ultimately limit the portfolio's growth potential.

Don't try to guess how far a stock can move up. If you do not give your stocks a lot of room to move upward, you will guarantee that your stock market profits will be below average.

### Pitfall 8: Shares Are Falling, but You Keep Buying

Some traders believe that shares that fall must retreat if technical triggers turn, that is, highlight that the share is oversold. In order to profit from such a strategy, you need to be simultaneously right about two things:

- The slide will end. The truth is some share do not stop falling until they are totally worthless.
- Timing of when and at what price the share's slide will end.

The novice trader often assumes that if a stock is near its 12-month low then it must therefore be in an opportune position to be bought. In addition, these traders convince themselves that buying such a share is not risky, because of that stock's low price relative to past earnings and book value. In reality, buying such a stock is always risky.

Traders must be aware that analysts' forecasts are based on sound knowledge, which includes discussions with management. So, if a stock is in a serious decline, it could be because market experts know some facts about the company's future earnings potential that the novice doesn't. Try looking at director dealings and, if these directors are selling their own shares, then you will understand why the share is in a downward spiral.

Keep in mind that a trader's objective is to maximize continuous profits, not to try and outsmart the market.

### Pitfall 9: Averaging Down

Adding to a losing position is simply too dangerous for the novice trader.

The reasoning in the mind of the investor is that the average cost per share will come way down once he or she adds to the position. This is called cost averaging, which is buying a certain amount into a stock at specified time intervals or at specified price intervals.

- **Time-Based Cost Averaging:** When an investor buys additional shares over equal time periods, such as $1,000 a month in Share A
- **Price-Based Cost Averaging:** When an investor invests an equal amount each time a stock declines in price by a certain percentage level

Over the past decade, I have used both systems and conclude that Time-Based Cost Averaging can work if done in a controlled manner. Price-Based Cost Averaging makes no sense in any circumstances and is sure to bankrupt you if practiced consistently. Usually, the trader sells his winning shares to buy more of the losing ones. If he or she continues to do this they will end up with a low priced losing stock, but one that is higher than the market price as he or she has been averaging down.

## Pitfall 10: Emotional Attachments

Some investors have a difficult time selling shares, because they have become emotionally attached, such as shareholders who have inherited shares and feel "guilty" in selling these. What your emotions tell you to do and what you should do are two different things.

It might be an obvious statement to state that a share can grow significantly over the years, but what many traders ignore is that a company will reach a stage of maturity and growth will slow, which in turn means that EPS will slow and consequently the share price will slow.

Therefore, traders must learn to *take profits* as success builds confidence, skill, and experience. However, you need to ensure that you find a balance between selling too soon and selling too late. This must be based on analysis and your actual stock performance and not, as some suggest, calculated guesswork.

Try to remain emotionally unattached to a stock so that you are not blinded to what the market is telling you about it.

## Pitfall 11: All Your Eggs in One Basket

The proverbial basket is made up in different ways. First, if you invest in only one share, then that investment is 100 percent at risk, in controllable and uncontrollable market forces. So, select a decent sample of shares. Remember that the more shares you have in a portfolio means additional and extensive analysis.

Second, when the basket consists of shares in only one sector, such as all mining companies, then—when the sector cycle changes, all your shares will be on the downswing.

Third, the basket is risk related, if you are risk averse, you should have more blue chip shares than middle caps or high risk. Too many in one sector exposes you to either low returns (blue chips) or higher risk (low-priced shares).

Last, the basket is focused on only one type of security, such as all equities or bonds. In this manner, the trader assumes additional risk of losing money in any given year as various securities are driven by different forces. It thus makes sense to keep some assets in each class to counterbalance the cyclical nature of markets.

### Pitfall 12: Everyone Is an Expert

Trading on advice without fundamental and technical analysis is pure guesswork. Remember that this is your career and not a hobby, so be professional.

### Pitfall 13: Get Rich Quick

Trying to beat the market is as old as time itself. Yet, it is important that this is not a poker match. You do not have to beat someone to make a profit. Keep your trades professional and to yourself.

Talking about your "wins" will not make you friends.

### Pitfall 14: Panic

Many traders panic at the first sign of a decline in the value of a specific share, while the professional sees a decline as an opportunity. **Once the preceding basic rules have become part of the traders' mindset, strategies have to be formed to select, buy, maintain, and sell shares.**

**Chapter 7 assesses the common traits, which most successful traders seem to have.**

# CHAPTER 7

# Common Traits of Successful Traders

*It's much easier to plan entry levels than to have an exit point.*

Assess and think about the following traits. These may not apply to you, but they are important to note.

## Basic Background

The following does not mean that if you do not meet these criteria, you cannot be a trader. These are simply observations.

| Trait | Details |
|---|---|
| Age | 25 and 35 years of age. |
| Marital status | Married or divorced, but seldom a bachelor. |
| Appearance | Dresses for comfort, with no ties. They have short hair and frequently have beards and moustaches. |
| Origins | Poor to middle-class homes: Poor homes drive some children to achieve more than their parents, while many wealthy move into family businesses. |
| Childhood | Absent parents can create an environment where children learn to live without a safety net, converted to entrepreneurial drive and perseverance. |
| Education | Many entrepreneurs are university dropouts, but driven not to disappoint those important to them (spouse, parents, and friends). |
| Other traits | Singly minded, focused, courageous, creative, insightful, and happy. |

## Personality Traits

### Trait 1: Confidence and Decisiveness

One of the most difficult traits to teach traders is one of confidence. I can teach you to be mechanical in your approach to trading, even build a staggering level of knowledge, but to be truly successful as a trader, you need to be able to absorb all teachings, skill, and experience and implement entry and exit strategies without hesitation and with the confidence that he or she has done the right thing.

As such, stated differently, it is this level of confidence that provides traders with power to make effective and decisive trading decisions. In fact, the jump from novice to professional trader will only happen when you can confidently learn from mistakes and have the courage to believe in your own convictions.

**Looking at this trait from a negative stance**: Lack or nil confidence tends to create doubt and indecision which, in turn, results in lack of timing trades, missed opportunities, and losses. Indecision really means that you don't truly believe in your skills.

### Trait 2: Positive Attitude

It is a truism that attitude improves with your experience and skills level. This, however, only takes place if you have developed a disciplined no-nonsense trading style that executes trades according to your predetermined and developed strategy. If you cannot execute your own signals, on both entry and exit signals, it takes just one mistake to give all those hard-earned profits back to the market.

It is an obvious statement to make, but belief in yourself and your trading skills is only built from being able to continuously achieve profits from the execution of your trading rules.

### Trait 3: Patience

This statement cannot be made enough: You don't have to trade every day. Your first question when you enter the trading day is not what you should trade, buy should you trade. Traders with patience and the discipline to follow their own trading rules know when to buy, sell, or stay out of the market. Losing because you are pressured to trade will ultimately end up with you losing your capital.

If you find that you are not conducting enough trades a week, then reassess your rules as they may be too severe or restrictive. These are your rules, so change them. Just don't go in the opposite direction and make the rules to lose.

### Trait 4: Discipline, Discipline, and More Discipline

This is the most critical trait and is discussed through these three volumes.

Simply stated, to be successful as a trader, be disciplined in all your stock trading activities, from research, following-up on portfolio management, ensuring that your capital is secured, assess and reassess technical triggers, and continuously improve your knowledge of international exchanges, markets, and industries.

### Trait 5: Be Passionate

It has been stated that people with passion love their work, don't look at their watches for the end of a work day, or are glad when weekends and public holidays arrive. Passionate people thoroughly enjoy reading charts, establishing and vigorously testing trading systems, dealing with financials, interpreting triggers, learning new strategies, and working on improving knowledge of environmental factors that affect markets.

### Trait 6: Acting Without Hesitation

Successful traders use time management effectively, knowing when to accept when they are wrong, accept failure and risk. They do this, assimilate the information, and move onto the next trade.

Essentially, traders take full responsibility for their actions, successes, and failures and the risks they took on when they set up their strategies. And they do this without hesitation.

### Trait 7: Take Total Responsibility

Every decision that you make is yours and yours alone.

**This must become your personal mantra.**

There is absolutely no other way to operate in a stock market. Always take trading action (buying or selling) only after you have conducted a corporate filter, undertaken fair value analysis and looked at technical triggers. There are those in the market that will insist that trading is 90 percent gut feel. For them this may be the case, but they also have to admit that they have been dealing in securities for many years and that "gut" feel has come with trading experience, losses, success, bull runs, and bear trends.

**Let's reiterate.** The successful trader knows every action he or she is about to take, every decision he or she will make, and only he or she is responsible for that action. You will seldom meet a successful trader who is looking to blame someone else for the consequences of their trading decisions. This simply does not happen.

## A Very Basic Concept

Once a trader accepts 100 percent responsibility for all actions, then he or she can learn from mistakes; noting in a trading journal the entry level, reasons for entry, and exit price. If a mistake was made, accept that you made a mistake, assess reasons for poor trading, and, more importantly, learn to not repeat those mistakes; at least, not too often.

There is not much that can be guaranteed in a stock market, but one issue is irrefutable. World famous market gurus do not blame market conditions, budget deficits, economic upheavals, political uncertainty, war on terrorism, emerging market imbalances, and technological change for making a loss in the market.

I have met traders who, after making a significant loss, have thrown their chairs against the wall, smashing expensive original paintings. However, when they have calmed down, they asked themselves:

- "Did I follow my own rules?" If the answer is yes, then they will look at their rules.
- Is there something that could be changed in their rules to avoid this loss again? Many times the answer will be an absolute "no." However, if the answer to the same question is "no" then some self-explanation will be called for. In many

instances, the trading rules will have been set down by the brokerage, so major losses caused from not following brokerage rules could result in dismissal.

For the independent trader, losses could result in personal insolvency and financial ruin. So, ask yourself the following questions:

- Why did I not follow rules, which I personally developed?
- How can I stop myself from doing that again?
- Am I likely to do that again?

Did you notice that the wording of the questions were all in the first person? Here the trader knows he or she takes total responsibility for every trade and is seeking reassurance that he or she will not break the rules again.

There's an old saying in trading: "If you have to ask whether you should trade—you shouldn't be trading." If you have a system that you have tested and proven over the long run that it does outperform the market and it is a system that fits your personal goals and strategy, why would you *ever* have to ask for an opinion? What extra will a third-party opinion provide? In fact, it will do nothing, but confuse you in making up your mind to trade.

This does not mean ignoring analysts' forecasts or changing market trends. It means that, if you have a trading strategy to buy only mining stocks, because that is your knowledge base and strength, then don't buy shares in furniture companies; no matter how attractive the share price may be. Another instance would be not to ask a day trader for advice if you believe in the long-term benefits of compounding.

If you *ever* find yourself wanting to ask a third party about your position, do the following:

- Close out the position (sell the security).
- Review your plan and rules.
- Work out why you lack the responsibility to follow your plan.
- When you are convinced you don't need a third party opinion start trading again.

How can a trader learn to accept total responsibility?

Have a set of rules and realize that the most important point in trading is following those rules. You have to be *disciplined and determined.* Once you have a set of firmly established rules you will find yourself not having to follow outside opinion. In fact, successful dealers go to great lengths not to listen to outside opinion.

| If the answer to the question *"Did I follow my rules?"* is: | |
|---|---|
| YES | Smile, despite the loss. You can learn from this loss, reviewing and changing your rules. This way you will ultimately become a winner. |
| NO | A reprimand is in order. You cannot know whether your rules work, if you don't follow them. You could end up making the same mistake repeatedly. |

Accept total responsibility for every trade you take from today and you'll be amazed at how easy trading ultimately becomes.

# Trading Traits

### Trait 1: Personalize Your Trading System

This sounds more complex than it really is.

Understand this: Every single successful trader, from every corner of the trading world, world has developed a trading methodology (some call it a *system)* that fits his or her personality and lifestyle. Some methodologies are developed over many years, some are extremely complex and computer generated, while some are simple, yet effective. It makes sense that a day trader would develop a system to identify patterns per hour, while long-term investors would be interested in developing systems to buy shares that are positive within 5-year up trends.

So, the ultimate methodology must be one that is developed and understood by you, and one that is effective in making profits for you. Don't hesitate. Start developing your personal trading system today by making copious notes on what you want and, more importantly, what you don't want. Ultimately, the way you trade must be intuitive enough to make profits—but also to avoid making loses.

More importantly, it must fit your unique personality.

The reason why many novice traders believe that such computer-based systems are better is simply because they have seeing such systems on television. In addition, during the past decade, trading companies have sprung up, marketing trading systems. Beware that such systems are expensive. Remember that these stockbroking systems are built to make thousands of deals for thousands of clients simultaneously.

Therefore, the system you need is a simple one to enable you to trade! Here is an example:

- In most exchanges you will find that companies are spread across numerous sectors.
- In fact, you will find that companies that should be in the same sector, sometimes are not.
- For instance, companies offering very similar services and products may be in the pharmaceutical sector or services sector.
- On way to create your own system is to find all these companies and create your own index. This way a change in the share price of one company within your personal pharm index will have a different percentage movement than in the exchange pharm index.
- This way you can assess the true effective movement in pharm companies and trade accordingly. For more information, write to me on jacques@bci.za.com.

I remember my old colleague at Global Capital, who used to, at the end of every day, say "today I made a profit, it was a great day!" Strangely, she would never say how much that profit was—or she was as happy if or she made $1 or $100,000. To her, not making a loss was her system of trading.

When asked if she would leave her trading career for another possibly more profitable one—her answer was always just a laugh. Most traders say that they cannot believe they were getting paid to do something they loved so much. So, you too could be saying similar things, but you will only be a top trader if you trade to a well-defined and personally developed system with established rules.

The question now therefore is: *How do you create a system that is personally tailored to suit you? I suggest that you start with a simple set of pertinent questions.*

Answer the following questions:

- How much trading profit do you expect to earn per year? Remember that anything below 15 percent is a loss, as you have to take into account capital gains tax, brokerage fees, and inflationary effects.
- Is trading a career or a hobby?
- Can you handle the stress that is inextricably linked to day trading?
- Will long-term trading be too boring for you?
- Will you tire of trading in the long term, that is, what is your attention span?
- Are you an action freak? Do you need daily action or do you prefer sitting behind a desk?
- Are you able to make continuous, rapid, and accurate decisions?
- Do you think out of the box? Can you identify trading opportunities without looking at a trading system?
- Can you take advice from a financial mentor, while you gain experience in trading?
- Have you read any trading books? How many? Do these inspire you to trade?
- Which trading style do you prefer and do you think that you could copy these trading styles?

## A Word of Warning

One of the biggest mistakes that many novice traders do is equate the need for trading funds with their ability to repay such funds. After all, if they take out a large mortgage, *will they be able to repay that loan with trading profits?* This belief stems from thinking that, if they can effectively emulate some famous day trader, *they will get rich; hopefully quickly.* Personally, I prefer to buy a share that I have analyzed thoroughly and hold it for at least 12 months. This period gives the company enough time to achieve forecasted goals and certainly enough time for at least one set of financial results to be released. This enables me to determine whether the company is, in fact, achieving its stated mission and publicized goals.

Over the past 4 years I have repeatedly proved how successful this method can be; at least, successful for clients who enjoy trading, but not too often.

If you are a novice or an unsuccessful trader then I suggest you start by asking yourself the following simple questions:

- Is there a trading style that suites my personality?
- What are these trading styles?
- Spend time to build a strong foundation so that your final trading system will be efficient and withstand difficult times; bear markets and daily volatility.
- If you build a weak foundation, your trading system will pull your capital into a bottomless pit.

This is where the majority of novice traders do go wrong.

Many traders have no idea which styles of trading suites them, so they keep changing from one style to another, often buying into the latest fashionable software in the hope that this will change their trading results. The problem is that losses often force novice traders out of the market before they find the systems that suites them. I believe any trader who can last over 2 years in the unpredictable world of trading could go on to become a successful trader; an independent trader.

**Usually, after 2 years these traders start to develop a set of rules that personally fits them. Their trading becomes more "comfortable" and profitable. The problem is that unfortunately, in their haste to make a ton of money, many traders will not get 2 years' experience before they lose their money or their interest. The hiring of a mentor in the early stages is important to establish a solid foundation.**

Get to work. There's a lot of crucial knowledge to be assimilated before a trading methodology can be properly developed.

### Trait 2: Plan Every Decision

There is no doubt that a novice trader will not last long in the market if he or she does not plan absolutely every trade he or she makes. As difficult as it is to believe, many new traders will buy shares in large amounts without blinking an eye and, to make matters worse, without undertaking *any* form of analysis. Imagine buying a house on the Internet without knowing where the property is located or how it is built?

**There is no point in even starting to create a trading plan if you are not logical or disciplined enough to follow it.**

You need to make the purchases based on logical and informed decisions, because once a trade has been made, there is no control as to where the share price will go. However, based on experience and skill, your personal trading system should have built in triggers to warn you to carry out predetermined strategies. This removes emotion out of the trading equation and should form the basis for systematic, professional, and stress-free trading.

The essence of having a plan is that it automates your trading strategy and removes the emotion out of trading. Thus, a strategy—or trading system—will set triggers to tell you at what price to buy a share and whether to sell the share if it climbs or falls.

A system of triggers will "professionalize" trading as it removes emotion. Under such conditions, the new trader does not have to have an opinion as to whether to buy a share, or panic if that share starts to fall. Even worse, greed in taking profits is just another trigger.

### Trait 3: Be Thorough

I have stated this before—stock markets are ruthless and have no favorites. The trading public is as likely to hit property sectors as they are to hammer commodities. As such, there will always be some event that could scare you to sell shares you didn't want to or some positive and momentous announcement to lure you to buy shares you had no intention of buying.

Only disciplined traders, who follow a well-designed and established plan, will survive this type of onslaught. If you are ever persuaded to trade or have to ask someone for an opinion as to whether you should buy, hold, or sell a share, then it can only be because:

- You have not designed and developed a trading plan.
- You have little faith in your plan or you have started to doubt your abilities.

The aforementioned example of buying a house without first seeing it is pertinent in highlighting how serious you should take planning your trading strategy. In the same manner as you would first investigate all aspects of the house on offer, the same amount of planning and effort should go into buying shares. After all, you may only have a small amount to trade today, but if your strategy is successful, you could be trading with much larger amounts in future.

As such, you must plan for positive, negative, and, more importantly, unforeseen events. Most of the time a trade will go your way and your plan will not have to be looked at, but what if the share suddenly rockets or falls like a stone, what should you do?

I cannot stress enough that complete discipline is crucial to succeed as a trader.

### Trait 4: Skills Can Always Be Refined

It's quite amazing that people from different walks of life believe that they can become traders overnight. When asked how long it took them to become chartered accountants, doctors, or plumbers, they seemed surprise at the question. Why do so many people expect to become market wizards within such a short period of time?

If you get to spend some time with successful traders such questions will not even surface, as you will very quickly realize just how much effort, time, determination, and planning it took to get to become traders for a living. To put it simply, being a successful stock market trader is not different to being a top lawyer, doctor, or entrepreneur.

In reality, traders go through years of trial and error and tremendous effort until they became consistent and successful traders. If you are a beginner, don't expect to strike out and make 80-percent returns in the first year of trading. A useful way of looking at trading as a career is to say that the first 3 years are time spent at university. The stock market is the teacher and your initial accounts are your fees.

So, what does it mean to work hard at your trading? Consider the following two sections:

- First you will have to spend much time on:
  - Self-analysis; understand your personality. Are you a risk taker or moderately risk averse?
  - Find a trading style that you are most comfortable with.
  - Learn how to trade properly; read, study, ask questions. Basically, you are going to have to start from scratch and build a system that fits you. It could take a couple of years, but it will be time well spent. If this sounds like too much effort, then you have just saved yourself a lot of lost money. Forget trading and move on to something which genuinely interests you. If doing solid ground works sounds good, and you can't wait to get started then you could have the talent to trader for a living.
- Once you have developed a trading system that fits you and you have the discipline to follow your plan then it is time to start trading. Start small and work up a portfolio that is well diversified.
- Understand that as a trader you will never quite get to a situation that you are completely satisfied with your trading skills. You must strive to keep improving. Never be satisfied with your trading system. This does not mean that you are always looking for faults with your trading system.
- Rather, every system and trading skill can be improved. The markets change all the time, so keep working on what influences new market developments could have on your trading system. Strive to become more disciplined and keep working on eliminating mistakes.

Only by controlling your emotions and working on your trading strategy will you avoid running into a trading catastrophes. How long does it take to become a competent trader? That depends of you and your determination to succeed.

# Developing Positive Attitude

Many portfolio managers that I have spoken to over the years have said: "Nothing helps you develop a great and positive attitude than seeing your portfolio grow." In other words, "seeing is believing."

Here is a little trick to get a true picture of your trading performance: Keep a track record of both current (open positions) as well as trades completed (shares bought and sold). Then take the two and combine them to see how well you have performed.

### *Basic Portfolio Maintenance*

Part 1: Overall Performance

| Figures in $ | Purchased Value | Current Value | % Difference |
|---|---|---|---|
| Portfolio (Open Positions) | 1,010,700.00 | 1,528,945.00 | 51.28 |
| Historic Trades (Closed Positions) | 679,625.00 | 1,134,620.00 | 66.95 |
| **Trading Performance** | **1,690,325.00** | **2,663,565.00** | **57.58** |

Part 2: Current Portfolio

| Company | Quantity | Cost Per Unit | Cost Total | Current Value Per Unit | Current Value Total | % Growth | % Of Portfolio |
|---|---|---|---|---|---|---|---|
| 1 | 6,000 | 1975 | 11,8625.00 | 2270 | 136,200.00 | 14.82 | 8.91 |
| 2 | 5,000 | 2800 | 14,0125.00 | 3870 | 193,500.00 | 38.09 | 12.66 |
| 3 | 4,500 | 3391 | 15,2720.00 | 6375 | 286,875.00 | 87.84 | 18.76 |
| 4 | 3,000 | 2961 | 88,955.00 | 3330 | 99,900.00 | 12.30 | 6.53 |
| 5 | 31,000 | 220 | 68,325.00 | 395 | 122,450.00 | 79.22 | 8.01 |
| 6 | 2,000 | 1550 | 31,125.00 | 4614 | 92,280.00 | 196.48 | 6.04 |
| 7 | 400,000 | 26 | 104,125.00 | 45 | 180,000.00 | 72.87 | 11.77 |
| 8 | 12,000 | 550 | 66,125.00 | 670 | 80,400.00 | 21.59 | 5.26 |
| 9 | 13,000 | 725 | 94,375.00 | 893 | 116,090.00 | 23.01 | 7.59 |
| 10 | 4,000 | 2430 | 97,325.00 | 3000 | 120,000.00 | 23.30 | 7.85 |
| 11 | 15,000 | 325 | 48,875.00 | 675 | 101,250.00 | 107.16 | 6.62 |
| Total | | | 1,010,700.00 | | 1,528,945.00 | 51.28 | 100.00 |

Part 3: Historic Portfolio

| Figures in $ | Quantity | Purchased | | Current Value | | % | 2016 |
|---|---|---|---|---|---|---|---|
| | | Price | Total | Price | Total | | |
| A | 7,000 | 2080 | 145,725.00 | 2995 | 209,650.00 | 43.87 | January 1 |
| B | 2,500 | 7975 | 199,500.00 | 10600 | 265,000.00 | 32.83 | January 21 |
| C | 170,000 | 29 | 49,425.00 | 50 | 85,000.00 | 71.98 | January 25 |
| D | 210,000 | 23 | 48,425.00 | 33 | 69,300.00 | 43.11 | March 10 |
| E | 160,000 | 39 | 62,525.00 | 75 | 120,000.00 | 91.92 | April 22 |
| F | 3,300,000 | 3 | 99,125.00 | 8 | 264,000.00 | 166.33 | June 15 |
| G | 41,000 | 86 | 35,385.00 | 136 | 55,760.00 | 57.58 | October 22 |
| H | 39,000 | 101 | 39,515.00 | 169 | 65,910.00 | 66.90 | November 28 |
| Total | | | 679,625.00 | | 1,134,620.00 | 66.95 | |

Let's review the previous portfolio:

The portfolio is split into three parts:

- **Part 1: Trading performance.** As a performance review to determine how he or she has performed in the market as a trader, you combine the current and historic performances. Here he or she achieved a 57.5 percent rise in the market.
- **Part 2: Open position.** This part outlines the current shares that the client has in the market. These cost him $1.01 million when he purchased the shares, including brokerage fees. The current value of the shares stands at $1.52 million, which is a growth of 51.28 percent.
  - o The last column shows the value of each share as a percentage of the whole portfolio.
  - o The client's personal rules were to have 10 shares at any one time, each constituting 10 percent of the portfolio. The rapid rise in Share 3 shares after the announcement of a possible buyout by a competitor has caused the portfolio imbalance.
  - o The strategy would be to follow personal rules and to sell Share 3, thus returning the portfolio to 10 shares. The imbalance would mostly correct itself.
- **Part 3: Historic portfolio.** This is portion of the portfolio that tells you where you have succeeded and failed. His

greatest success was with Share F (+166%) and his most
disappointing was the sale of Share B (+32%). The client
sold the share at this level because the share retracted at that
point, falling by 5 percent over a 5-day period. The sale was
disappointing because the share rose rapidly from that level
to touch the $130 mark. However, the client had kept to
his strategy of placing a 5-percent stop loss on shares that
rose by more than 30 percent, which he kept strictly to. No
wonder the history portion of his portfolio looks a healthy
67 percent up.

Traders can use the aforementioned structure to boost their positive
attitudes as traders.

It must be stressed that it does take years of experience for traders to
develop the belief that they can achieve solid results over a long period.
Trade with such a small risk in the early years that it hardly seems worth
your while. View trading as a career and not a "get rich quick scheme."

**The confidence lesson: You will have achieved total confidence in
your trading abilities only when you see your portfolio in percentages rather than in money**

One client asked: "How can you do that when it's money we are trading with?"

The only answer is: *discipline.*

Checking how much money you've made or lost each day is emotionally draining. No one can succeed like this. The percentages tell you
whether you should buy more shares, sell existing shares (or reduce a
holding), or whether you should just wait—according to your own rules?
Top traders do not see markets as a cash box, but simply as a way of operating a business.

- **Notes and recommendations.** If you have a financial mentor,
  this is where he or she would place a recommendation. In this
  instance, the financial advisor could suggest that the client
  wait until the listing of a new company to acquire additional
  shares.

If emotions are potent destroyers of successful trading, then common sense dictates that to be a successful trader you must eliminate all emotion from trading. How is this done? Once again, discipline to follow the rules.

Be robotic. Be disciplined. The money will take care of itself.

**Part 3, Chapter 8 highlights the critical need to manage your finances before you start to trade.**

# PART III
# Portfolio Structures

# CHAPTER 8

# Money Management Before Trading

*It's never too early to start.*

## Success in Trading Depends on Money Management

Savings to securities flow chart

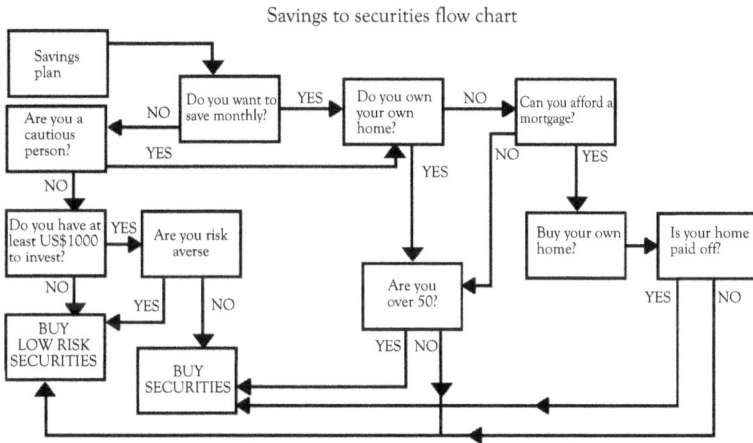

So far, we have been laying the foundations for share trading. So, this is the final section to get you ready for trading. Please bear with me as this section is extremely important and must be taken seriously before you become a trader. Understand that savings and a savings plan is a long term commitment and a necessary one for you to prosper as a trader. The main difficulty with long-term saving is that inflation is an unknown variable.

If we could be sure that prices are going to rise at an average rate of 4 percent a year over the next 20 years, this difficulty would not exist: you could, for instance, put all your money into well-chosen bonds or index stocks, giving a profit of 8 percent a year. All you need is 7.5 percent annual return to double your money, but with an inflation rate of 4 percent it would effectively take you 20 years to double your funds.

In effect, the actual buying power of your money would only increase by 50 percent in just over 10 years, and would more than double in 20 years.

And if inflation averaged 10 percent a year, you would be able to buy only about 66 percent as much with your money after 20 years as you could have done when you saved it up, which isn't a very appealing prospect.

For long-term saving, you need something that will stand a chance of keeping up and being higher than inflation, whatever heights it may reach—and this basically means something which is directly linked to the value of money.

There are three kinds of investment which, in the past, have met this need: ordinary shares of companies, which you buy on the stock exchange; houses and land; and valuable things such as certain paintings, antiques, and so on.

These volumes concentrate on the acquisition of shares. What this means is that, if you are saving for the long term, you have to spread your risk as widely as possible, so that, if one of the shares you have chosen does very badly, you don't lose everything.

There are two stock exchange maxims, which have more than a grain of truth in it, which says: *The small investor is always wrong* and *how did I make a small fortune in the market? I started out with a large fortune.*

When you are saving for the long term, you have to choose something which stands a chance of coping with inflation—however bad inflation may become. This basically means that you have to be prepared to take risks, since the only things which are flexible enough to cope with inflation have no fixed value themselves: you have to rely on their value going up to give you the profit you need.

The stock exchange is one answer though buying stocks. If you want to put money on the stock exchange, you have three main choices: higher risk securities (shares and derivatives) and lower risk unit trusts, which can also fluctuate, but which are more stable.

If you want to invest direct in equities, you should aim to spend at least $200 to $300 on the shares of each company you choose a month:

any less than that, and dealing charges start to become unduly expensive. If you also want to stand a reasonable chance of keeping your money safe, you will have to have a spread of shares; at least 10, carefully selected and spread among a number of different industries.

Buying shares in unit trusts will not need so much money, as your risk is already spread among a range of shares. Buying units in a unit trust needs less money, since the dealing charges are built into the buying and selling price of each unit and so are not prohibitively expensive on small amounts. Unit trusts are also safer, and have the advantage that you can save up regularly. But, on average, profits are not as good as those of securities.

## Successful Investors Start with Savings

What do you do if you're a trader who has not been able to trade for the entire month; *whatever the reason may be?* Novice traders tend to believe that once they understand some technical triggers and have opened up an online trading account, their careers start. Few novice traders are really prepared for difficult time. Some have told me that they can simply sell shares to pay expenses. Doing that means that you are reducing your trading capital. It also means that the next month you will have less capital to achieve the same goals. So, you will have to employ a higher risk strategy as you have less cash. Imagine that the following month is December and now you have fewer days to trade, face liquidity problems as professional; dealers take the Christmas break. Panic sets in and you take greater and riskier chances.

The end of that trader's career is transparent.

There is only one way to attain financial security, as a trader and as a self-employed worker. Take heed before you face the reality that no work means no pay. To succeed therefore means that you have both a savings and a trading account. Ensure that you have your at least 6 months' "salary" saved before you begin to trade.

Repeatedly, I have met the ultrawealthy traders, but also people who live modestly. They have funds that they trade and savings to meet their monthly expenses. They also go on holiday and their modest living gives them comfort that they are doing what they love for a living, which they do without panic.

*Three Simultaneous Steps*

You need to assess and develop a strategy for the following:

- Develop a financial plan with budgets.
- Establish a payment plan for high-interest debt.
- Set out timeframes for saving and investing.

## Develop a Financial Plan with Budgets

There are literally thousands of books on budgets and how to easily accomplish financial goals. It is sufficient to state that you need to make a comprehensive list of expenses. Leave nothing out and then add a buffer for miscellaneous and unforeseen expenses.

Include in your list, among other, cost of mortgage, vehicle leasing, education, medical, and other insurance and holidays.

Once your list has been completed, prioritize the items and then set a timeframe to fulfill each goal. You need to do this as the first step in your trading will be to meet these goals with the appropriate trading risk profile.

## Savings and High Interest Debt

There is an economic principle that states that you shouldn't pay off your high interest bearing debt before you commence to trade. The reason is that, under an inflationary environment, the debt is effectively reduced as cost of money becomes less. Under such conditions you would have to calculate the real effect of your debt on your savings or trading or both.

As follows:

- Debt = 6 percent interest
- Savings = 4 percent interest
- Inflation = 2 percent

If you had $1,000 in debt and the same amount in savings, should you use the savings to pay off the debt? Remember that savings form part of your long-term trading plan. So, if inflation diminishes real debt, but also real returns, then look at the following using simplistic interest over 12 months.

- Debt = $1,000 \times 0.06$ = Total debt of $1,060;
- Savings = $1,000 \times 0.04$ = Total savings of $1,040;
- Interest on debt is higher than savings, therefore—while inflation affects both—it has more of an impact on the higher debt.

The issue isn't an economic one, but one of practical efficiencies. For instance, you don't really know whether inflation will rise or not. So, you must calculate whether your potential return in the market will enable you to meet these expenses or not.

Let's end the chapter by saying that trading is obviously higher risk than a bank savings account. While you can lose your capital, you can certainly gain a greater percentage return with trading than the safe haven of banking your funds.

**Chapter 9 is an overview of how to start your investment and trading career.**

# CHAPTER 9

# The Early Years

*Keep to your own strategy: Hesitation results in missing the opportunity.*

**This chapter outlines an overall strategy to start your trading career and, second, it looks at pertinent issues that affect markets, which are often missed by novice traders. The latter is a set of basic money management points to acknowledge.**

## Your First Years of Trading

### Starting Your Trading Career

Year 1: Get Organized

- Work on establishing whether you can (or are willing to) put the time and effort into developing a system that not only works, but also fits your personality and risk averseness.
- Start by acquiring and reading basic books on stock markets and trading.
- Attend as many seminars as you can. Stay away from those that claim that they will reveal secrets to stock market wealth. Go to seminars about basic chart reading skills, psychology of trading, and portfolio management.
- Using a very simple charting package, start looking at some bar charts of shares and the markets. Start to build a foundation of technical knowledge.

The easiest is to get a share mentor, who will guide you through the first year, helping you to set up structures, understand the basics of investing, build confidence, and assist you in setting up databases. Contact me on mentor@magliolo.com for such assistance.

**At the end of Year 1, you should know whether trading is for you**. You should also have worked out what kind of trading technique appeals to you. Remember that you can change your system of trading over time, as you gain knowledge, skill, and experience.

If you find trading is not for you, you have saved a lot of time and money. This does not mean that you cannot invest in the stock market. Use a mentor to trade for you, using your personality traits.

Year 2: Start Trading

- **Open an online brokerage trading account with a small amount of cash.** These are your learning fees. Expect to lose it all as part of your fees. However, a mentor could assist you in this when you start out (Year 1).
- Keep reading, studying, attending seminars, and asking your mentor questions—specific to trading, and also general economics.
- Develop a style of trading with which you are comfortable. Trading with a small amount of cash will not make you rich, but it will give you a greater understanding of trading techniques and invaluable lessons on entry and exit levels. Keep a journal with all the details of your trades, which will assist you when you analyze your performances.
- Develop a money management and trading plan. Try to accommodate for every possibility.
- Keep observing the charts and start a virtual trading portfolio. Remember that virtual trading can be misleading, as no emotions play a part of such trading.
- Start buying stocks in different amounts (share prices between 1 cent and 100 cents) and see how these trades change the profile of each investment relative to the whole portfolio. This should teach you the significance of portfolio management.

**Example:** If you have five shares worth an equal amount in your portfolio, then each share represents 20 percent of your portfolio. If two of these shares are high risk, then 40 percent of your portfolio is based on daily potential trades, while 60 percent of your portfolio is less risk averse.

Now, if one of the three shares that make up your lower risk portion of your portfolio drops in price, you could end up with 50 percent high risk and 50 percent less risk. What should you do to return the value of the overall portfolio back to a 40:60 ratio?

The answer will be different for each trader. Traders could sell one of the less risk averse shares, sell the share that has dropped in price, or reduce the quantity of the shares being held.

If you feel comfortable trading, then make a trade. The whole point of trading is to follow your own developed rules. Making or losing money is not the important point as this stage. Trade with such a small amount hardly seems worthwhile. What you want to know is:

- How do you react when the value of shares fall?
- Can you follow your own rules?
- Is this system working?

Year 3: Refine Your Trading System

- You should have your own system that fits you and you should be making profits.
- If you still find yourself lacking the discipline to follow the signals (as set out by your own rules), ask why?
- By now, if you are still trading, you should be making consistent profits in the market and continue learning. Now is the time to diversify your portfolio into the derivative market, such as spread trading, forex, and warrants.
- If you want to be a top trader there's a lot of work involved. Do not be fooled by all the trade magazines saying you can achieve 100 percent a year with no effort. If you really do keep working at it the rewards can be amazing.

## Money Management Lessons

### Lesson 1: Plan From the Start

The first lesson to be learnt from the aforementioned is to start investing early.

It is not always possible to do this, but remember that the earlier you start, the easier the burden. In addition, you are more likely to have a successful outcome. In fact, it is never too early to invest for retirement, but it can get too late.

It is extremely easy to put off retirement planning; there is always a good excuse, so be aware and try not to let it happen to you. The cost of reaching your goal does go up each day.

### Lesson 2: Aim for a Reasonable Rate of Return

Getting a reasonable rate of return on investments depends on an individual's perception, the country of origin, place of investment, and risks attached to the investment. While 10 percent may be a fair rate in the United States, in emerging markets it would be a little more than breaking-even if inflation is taken into account.

In addition, far too much money is committed to safe and low-risk securities, like unit trusts, and too little to the higher risk, higher return classes. The latter doesn't mean reckless trading, but starting with equities. If you want to be a trader, then you start with shares and work your way to trading derivatives. So, start with a target percentage return as a goal, which you can change over the years as you gain experience and skill.

Remember the simple rule is that you can double your money every 10 years with a low-risk interest rate of 7.5 percent. In the following example, a capital amount of $1,000 is invested for 10 years and the interest is reinvested. In the investment decade the capital rises to $2,061.03.

| Year | Capital | Interest @7.5%) | Total |
|---|---|---|---|
| 1 | 1,000.00 | 75.00 | 1,075.00 |
| 2 | 1,075.00 | 80.63 | 1,155.63 |
| 3 | 1,155.63 | 86.67 | 1,242.30 |
| 4 | 1,242.30 | 93.17 | 1,335.47 |
| 5 | 1,335.47 | 100.16 | 1,435.63 |
| 6 | 1,435.63 | 107.67 | 1,543.30 |
| 7 | 1,543.30 | 115.75 | 1,659.05 |
| 8 | 1,659.05 | 124.43 | 1,783.48 |
| 9 | 1,783.48 | 133.76 | 1,917.24 |
| 10 | 1,917.24 | 143.79 | 2,061.03 |

Given that risk in an equity portfolio falls as time horizon increases, traders should consider shifting assets to where they will get higher rates of return as the timeframe reduces. That means fewer bonds, unit trusts and annuities, and more shares.

Within the share classes, research indicates that a higher percentage of funds should go to value companies, small-cap shares, international hedge stocks, and emerging markets. These will increase rates of return. Properly mixed, these asset classes should generate significantly higher than 10 percent returns without undue risk.

In addition, as your skills increase, you will be able to move in the higher reward-risk securities of derivatives. In addition, move your target markets to new regions, thus diversifying your portfolio to different economic trends and cycles.

### Lesson 3: Don't Forget Costs

When many portfolio managers talk about return, the one negative aspect they tend to concentrate on is risk. Yet cost can also have a major impact on investment goals. Markets are reasonably efficient and it is unlikely that you can beat them by much over time, especially when you take costs into account. In a global investment plan, with the many risks and costs attached, be careful not to have costs that exceed returns.

### Lesson 4: Control Taxes

One of the least understood costs in a trading or investment portfolio is how tax can become crippling if not properly managed. Each time we receive an interest payment or you sell your shares at a profit, you are liable to paying a portion of interest or profits in tax. In addition, many countries have additional taxes such as capital gains tax and taxes on dividends received.

In a number of instances, such taxes can be deferred to another time. So, the aim is to have funds to reinvest and earn compounding interest before paying the tax.

The following example highlights the concept of real compound growth:

- K Lorry and R Blank both have $100,000 to invest a year for 3 years.
- Both Lorry and Blank intend to invest the money with a bank at an annual compound growth rate of 10 percent.
- Both investors are in the highest tax bracket, which equates to 30 percent tax on all interest received.
- Lorry prefers to remove the interest yearly, while Blank intends to withdraw the full interest at the end of the third year.

**Tax liability:**
**A. Lorry (withdraws interest annually)**

| Years | Invest-ment | Interest received* | Total | With-draw | Tax liability | Net balance |
|---|---|---|---|---|---|---|
| Year 1 | $100,000.00 | $10,471.30 | $110,471.30 | $10,471.30 | $3,141.39 | $100,000.00 |
| Year 2 | $100,000.00 | $10,471.30 | $110,471.30 | $10,471.30 | $3,141.39 | $100,000.00 |
| Year 3 | $100,000.00 | $10,471.30 | $110,471.30 | $10,471.30 | $3,141.39 | $100,000.00 |
| TOTAL | $100,000.00 | $31,413.90 | $131,413.90 | $31,413.90 | $9,424.17 | $100,000.00 |

**Conclusions:**

- Lorry earned $31,413.90 in interest and paid $9,424,17 in taxes.
- This means that his investment has earned him a net $21,989.73.
- This equates to a 22-percent net return over 3 years.

**B. Blank (withdraws interest at the end of the 3-year investment period)**

| Years | Invest-ment | Interest received* | Total | With-draw | Tax liability | Net balance |
|---|---|---|---|---|---|---|
| Year 1 | $100,000.00 | $10,471.30 | $110,471.30 | - | - | $110,471.30 |
| Year 2 | $110,471.30 | $11,567.79 | $122,039.09 | - | - | $122,039.09 |
| Year 3 | $122,039.09 | $12,779.09 | $134,818.18 | $34,818.18 | $10,445.45 | $100,000.00 |
| TOTAL | $100,000.00 | $34,818.18 | $134,818.18 | $34,818.18 | $10,445.45 | $100,000.00 |

**Conclusions:**

- Blank earned $34,818.18 in interest and paid $10,445.45 in taxes.

- This means his investment has earned him a net $24,372.73.
- This equates to a 24.37-percent net return over 3 years.

---

**\* Formula for compound interest:**

$$T = D\,(1+(\text{interest}/12))^{n\times12}$$

Where:
- T = Total investment, which is the capital amount plus interest received
- D = Monthly investment deposit
- N = Period of years that the investment is to take place. This is multiplied by the compounded period. In this case by 12 months. Note that interest is divided by the same amount, that is, if the interest was compound daily, interest would be divided by 365 days and "n" would be multiplied by 365.

---

So, who is better off?

- While Lorry paid marginally less tax, his overall investment return is less than Owen's. This is a result of annual withdrawals, which inhibited the compound effect on a higher annual amount (interest on the previous year's interest).
- While both paid a 30 percent tax rate on interest, as a percentage of the total value of investments at the end of the 3-year period, Lorry paid less tax. This is due to the effect that $100,000 has on a small investment amount, compared to the much larger final portfolio of Blank.

# Compounding

**An example:**
Suppose that for 10 years, you deposit $1,000 into an account at a 10-percent rate of interest. Your investment will grow to $15,937.42 by the 10th year. At this point, you stop making contributions and you intend to leave this investment for your child's retirement. In other words, the cash will remain in the bank at 10 percent for the next 55 years. The fund will grow to $3 million over that period.

To adjust for inflation, we assume that about 3.5 percent of the nominal yield was eroded. The "real value" of the accumulation in terms of dollars at the start of the investment process is $322,027.60. The "real value" of the inflation-adjusted income available to you is $20,931.79 for the rest of your life. We are assuming that you withdraw 6.5 percent beginning at age 65, and leave 3.5 percent to grow to hedge the inflation rate. All of this was accomplished with a total cost of only $10,000.

Compounding had worked its magic.

Now let's assume that $1,000 is deposited a year for 55 years. This will accumulate $1,880,591.43 for your child's retirement. If you waited 10 years before you started with the deposits, you would lose $1.2 million.

Stated differently, if you want to still accumulate $3,013,115.83, a total of $1,602.22 per year must be contributed for 55 years at 10 percent. The total cost of the program has grown to $88,121.94.

Let us change the example again. You are 20 years old, just out of school, and want to save for your retirement. How much must you save each year at 10 percent to accomplish the same goal at age 65? The answer is that it will take $4,191.26 per year. The price is going up, but it is not yet out of reach.

What happens if you wait even later?

- At age 30 the annual cost of meeting your goal has grown to $11,117.51 a year.
- At age 40 there are 25 years remaining to age 65 and your cost to fund your retirement supplement is now $30,637.58 per year.
- Age 50 means there are only 15 years to go until your planned retirement, but you will need to deposit $94,823.14 each year to achieve your targeted retirement fund.
- Age 60 finds that $189,059.14 is required each year to fund your retirement plan and it is clearly out of the question. Many people find themselves in this situation and the common reaction is to wonder how it will feel to still be working at 80.
- **There is another alternative.** Investors can also withdraw annual interest received, pay the tax on the interest and reinvest the funds back into the same institution. However, the benefit of doing this is marginal.

| Figures in U.S. dollars | OPTION 1 No annual withdrawal | OPTION 2 Withdraw interest annually | | OPTION 3 Withdraw interest, pay taxes and reinvest remaining sum | | | |
|---|---|---|---|---|---|---|---|
| | Capital + Interest | Interest | Annual Tax | Capital | Interest | Tax | Amount to reinvest |
| Year 1 | 110,471.31 | 10,471.31 | 3,141.393 | 100,000 | 10,471.31 | 3141.3918 | 7,329.9142 |
| Year 2 | 122,039.09 | 10,471.31 | 3,141.392 | 107,329.9 | 11,238.84 | 3371.653124 | 7,867.190622 |
| Year 3 | 134,818.18 | 10,471.31 | 3,141.392 | 107,867.2 | 11,295.1 | 3388.531081 | 7,906.572523 |
| Year 4 | 148,935.41 | 10,471.31 | 3,141.392 | 107,906.6 | 11,299.23 | 3389.768221 | 7,909.459182 |
| Year 5 | 164,530.89 | 10,471.31 | 3,141.392 | 107,909.5 | 11,299.53 | 3389.858902 | 7,909.670772 |
| Year 6 | 181,759.42 | 10,471.31 | 3,141.392 | 107,909.7 | 11,299.55 | 3389.865549 | 7,909.686281 |
| Year 7 | 200,792.01 | 10,471.31 | 3,141.392 | 107,909.7 | 11,299.55 | 3389.866036 | 7,909.687418 |
| Year 8 | 221,817.55 | 10,471.31 | 3,141.392 | 107,909.7 | 11,299.55 | 3389.866072 | 7,909.687501 |
| Year 9 | 245,044.75 | 10,471.31 | 3,141.392 | 107,909.7 | 11,299.55 | 3389.866075 | 7,909.687507 |
| Year 10 | 270,704.13 | 10,471.31 | 3,141.392 | 107,909.7 | 11,299.55 | 3389.866075 | 7,909.687508 |
| Year 11 | 299,050.39 | 10,471.31 | 3,141.392 | 107,909.7 | 11,299.55 | 3389.866075 | 7,909.687508 |
| Year 12 | 330,364.87 | 10,471.31 | 3,141.392 | 107,909.7 | 11,299.55 | 3389.866075 | 7,909.687508 |
| Year 13 | 364,958.39 | 10,471.31 | 3,141.392 | 107,909.7 | 11,299.55 | 3389.866075 | 7,909.687508 |
| Year 14 | 403,174.30 | 10,471.31 | 3,141.392 | 107,909.7 | 11,299.55 | 3389.866075 | 7,909.687508 |
| Year 15 | 445,391.91 | 10,471.31 | 3,141.392 | 107,909.7 | 11,299.55 | 3389.866075 | 7,909.687508 |

(Continued)

(Continued)

| Figures in U.S. dollars | OPTION 1 No annual withdrawal | OPTION 2 Withdraw interest annually | | OPTION 3 Withdraw interest, pay taxes and reinvest remaining sum | | | |
|---|---|---|---|---|---|---|---|
| | Capital + Interest | Interest | Annual Tax | Capital | Interest | Tax | Amount to reinvest |
| Year 16 | 492,030.26 | 10,471.31 | 3,141.392 | 107,909.7 | 11,299.55 | 3389.866075 | 7,909.687508 |
| Year 17 | 543,552.25 | 10,471.31 | 3,141.392 | 107,909.7 | 11,299.55 | 3389.866075 | 7,909.687508 |
| Year 18 | 600,469.27 | 10,471.31 | 3,141.392 | 107,909.7 | 11,299.55 | 3389.866075 | 7,909.687508 |
| Year 19 | 663,346.25 | 10,471.31 | 3,141.392 | 107,909.7 | 11,299.55 | 3389.866075 | 7,909.687508 |
| Year 20 | 732,807.26 | 10,471.31 | 3,141.392 | 107,909.7 | 11,299.55 | 3389.866075 | 7,909.687508 |
| Year 21 | 809,541.76 | 10,471.31 | 3,141.392 | 107,909.7 | 11,299.55 | 3389.866075 | 7,909.687508 |
| Year 22 | 894,311.35 | 10,471.31 | 3,141.392 | 107,909.7 | 11,299.55 | 3389.866075 | 7,909.687508 |
| Year 23 | 987,957.43 | 10,471.31 | 3,141.392 | 107,909.7 | 11,299.55 | 3389.866075 | 7,909.687508 |
| Year 24 | 1,091,409.47 | 10,471.31 | 3,141.392 | 107,909.7 | 11,299.55 | 3389.866075 | 7,909.687508 |
| Year 25 | 1,205,694.30 | 10,471.31 | 3,141.392 | 107,909.7 | 11,299.55 | 3389.866075 | 7,909.687508 |

- The preceding factors become more pronounced over the longer term. This is highlighted by the following three investment options.
- For the best advice on tax, which includes among others, forming a closed corporation, trust account, other types of firm, it is best to consult a tax expert, who can advise you about offshore funds and tax implications of investing in other countries.

| Summary | OPTION 1 | OPTION 2 | OPTION 3 |
|---|---|---|---|
| Capital + Interest | $1,205,694.30 | $361,782.7 | $381,595.1 |
| Total interest | $1,105,694.30 | $261,782.7 | $281,595.1 |
| Tax | $331,708.29 | $78,534.8 | $84,478.52 |
| Net income | $773,986.01 | $183,247.9 | $197,116.6 |
| Tax as % of interest | 30.0% | 30.0% | 30.0% |
| As % of interest + Capital | 27.5% | 21.71% | 22.14% |

**Comment:** The best way to ensure that the investor has the funds when he or she needs them is to set up an automatic monthly deduction, e.g., stop or debit order. This will put the tremendous power of compounding to work and reinforce decisions to start sooner than later. Above all else, the trader and investor must start as early as possible, but where not possible, then customize your strategy to meet your financial goals.

**Part 4, Chapter 10 discusses how to become a street smart trader.**

# PART IV

# Streetwise versus Experts

# CHAPTER 10

# Be Street Smart

*If your analysis is wrong, don't wait, get out.*

In setting up a trading strategy and portfolio you need to consider a balance between technical triggers and fundamental issues that influence markets and shares. The first relates to portfolio structures, asset allocation, and your rules for entering and exiting stock positions; and the second relates to an understanding of risk-reward factors, financials and corporate structures, and governance. I would like to add a third factor, which I call *Streetwise Fundamentals*.

These are issues that assess managerial capabilities, shareholder rights, understanding the reflective mood of traders, and economics and politics which are issues that cannot really be quantified. These are factors that make the astute investor more streetwise.

Therefore, in building a strong strategy it is essential to have a sound understanding of all three factors. The analysis of financial data and technical triggers are set out in out later volumes and, therefore, the following text deals with issues relevant to streetwise preparedness. This is followed by variables that will assist you to build a better benchmark for yourself.

## The Streetwise Trader

Over time, if the investor is wise, he or she will gain experiences in understanding how people behave in the market and what such behavior influences trading patters; *at times rational and then completely illogical.* After all, there are many traders who have no understanding of financials, yet they make buy and sell decisions on gut feel and sentiment. These decisions, in turn, affects overall investor mood and thus share prices. There is however a real thread of logic that can be applied to understanding the masses of faceless traders.

The following text points out some nonmathematical methods and issues to consider when taking investor sentiment into account.

## Management

For most traders, getting hold of the managers or directors of a listed company is near impossible. Since speaking to them is difficult, there must, therefore, be an alternative method to assess the effectiveness of these directors.

In 2014, a stockbroker and I interviewed the directors of a Cape Town-based food listed company. The directors said that "everything is positive," and "we can achieve 25 percent growth this year." Despite their attempts at conveying a positive message, they seemed uneasy.

After the discussion, my colleague turned to me and said that he was going back to the office to advice clients to continue to accumulate the share. He then asked me for my advice.

This is what I said: "I believe that the company is about to be delisted, with head office using this company to reverse list another operation, possibly the Johannesburg-based holding company."

He looked at me, slightly confused and, shaking his head, asked me how I had concluded that scenario. Simply, the directors had avoided any question relating to head office, which immediately made me suspicious. In addition, having gathered the necessary information on the company prior to the interview I knew:

- Head office was planning to move other food operations into Africa. They would need a listed vehicle to fund such a venture.
- Head office was not content with the bad publicity that the Cape Town-listed company had received in the recent past.
- Part of the holding company's plans (announced in the press) was to "take greater control over our subsidiaries to unite us in a single, focused mission."

Within 3 weeks of my statement to my colleague, the holding company announced a delisting of the Cape Town firm. I had proved my statement to institutional clients, yet all it took was gut feel and listening closely. In other words, try to know that people often say more by not speaking at all.

If you are "listening" you can get an investment edge or, stated differently, learn to read between the lines.

### IPO and Long-Term Strategy

Here is a truism. An IPO has no trading history, so the masses of traders need to be convinced that your share price is fair and has a chance of providing them with reasonable capital growth over the next 12 months.

Forecasts are set out in the IPO's prospectus and, subsequently, in annual reports.

An important part of the prospectus or annual report is the mission statement, often ignored by traders. The directors use this statement to bring traders, investors, and staff together with a focused, common ideology and direction.

Your assessment of the mission statement must look at two issues:

- **Is this statement too broad?** A statement should be broad enough to allow an understanding that the company is focused and driven with a common goal or mission.
- **Is this statement focused?** It should be focused enough to provide individuals with clear understanding of the company's future direction. Often these statements ignore the labor force. A solid mission statement can keep workers and employers united and avoid strike action, loss of productivity and avoid a falling share price.

A broad statement is effective blue sky planning or brainstorming. A statement that is too restricted foregoes future opportunities.

However, trading in IPOs is seriously misunderstood and also massively missed opportunities. If you can place a value on the share from the prospectus info, then you could acquire the share as a short-term strategy.

Take note:

- The share price stated on the prospectus is not the share price at listing. So, if you assess that the current trend in IPO offers is twice oversubscribed, then make an offer for twice what you want. For instance, if you want to buy $10,000.00 of the IPO, then offer $20,000.
- The listing price is determined by the book building method of listing. So, if the prospectus offer price is $10 per share, if the mutual and other funds bid the share to $20, then the broker will calculate a price on a formula. In this case the listing price would be about $15 a share.
- Understand that you received the shares at $10.
- The first 3 days of an IPO listing often sees a price move by 25 percent. This is called Abnormal Initial Return. A system to entice mutual funds to acquire the share.
- If you invested $10,000 at $10 per share, you would have received 1,000 shares.
- At listing these go up by 25 percent, giving you a share value of $18.75.
- You have effectively bought the share at $10 and now it is $18.75. This is a profit of 87.5 percent.
- See Appendix for further explanation.

Whether you hold the share for the future or not, trading in IPOs can be profitable. There are numerous strategies that can be adopted, so send me a message if you are interested: jacques@bci.za.com

## Market and Industry Characteristics

Another nonmathematical method of determining whether a company has a suitable strategy is to conduct fundamental research and analysis that a company faces in the environmental factors within which it operates; including, politics, economics, finance, global threats and opportunities, technology, social change, and labor issues.

The dilemma traders and investors face is what factors to include and exclude when setting up key criterion for trading decision making. One approach is to create a filter system; set out in later volumes.

Among the research techniques used by analysts are: understanding key value triggers, SWOT analysis of the industry and of the company, Pestle analysis, and conducting Porters Five Forces (see Appendixes for an explanation of the latter two).

Some key filters include an assessment of overall markets, peer analysis, market fragmentation, director entrepreneurial flair, and possible synergies arising out of acquisitions, merger, and expansion of product range or region. Stated differently, a company must show in its performance that it is meeting and complying with its mission statement.

## Identifying Winners at a Glance

If it is assumed that the board of directors is responsible for the direction, growth, and future prospects of a company, it is fair to assume that a comparison of that company relative to its sector index—for a set period—is valid. This test of management's ability is extremely broad.

For instance, not all pharmaceutical companies within the sector of an exchange buy, sell, or produce the same products. One company may be strong in the export market, another may be labor intensive and yet another may have a spread of divisions to include hospitals.

In addition, not all pharmaceutical companies listed on an exchange would be listed in the pharmaceutical sector. Some may be listed under the services sector, because it has logistical transport services.

The most effective way to identify winners in a sector is to create your own sector. Database these companies and create an index using these companies' market cap. The total market cap becomes the index. So, if you have 10 companies in this "created" sector, you will find that movement in the companies that make up the Index will have a different comparable movement to that shown in the official statistics.

These would be different, but would provide you with information that is unique to your trading strategy.

## Analyzing the Winners: Random Theory Approach

Is it possible to conclude that companies that beat the sector averages are wise and others are not? By extension, can the people who invested with companies that outperformed the indexes also claim to be winners? Is it possible that these winners could have been predicted? A truism in statistical analysis is that probability theory will always account for a number of winners and losers in any random series of events.

The example often used to demonstrate probability theory is, if one person tosses a coin 100 times to get "heads," is it likely that he will succeed 50 times? Actually, there is no guarantee that the more times the coin is thrown, the greater his chances are of getting the desired result. Every time he throws, he has an equal chance of success, but also an equal chance of failure.

If it is assumed that markets are efficient, it can be expected that a random distribution of results will show there are some winners and also some losers. Therefore, how does an investor know which director to trust, who to follow, and how much to invest in that company?

The answer is never easy and there is a multitude of ways to assess the situation:

- **In an efficient market there are large numbers of buyers and sellers**, which means that market perception of a directors' ability is reflected in the share price. For instance, if the company does not perform, or the directors are involved in a scandal, investors are likely to sell the shares. A large volume of sales often sends the share price downwards. After all, nobody wants to invest in a company that does badly.
- **To offset the problem of number distortions, use growth averages rather than direct comparisons.** For instance, instead of comparing the 2017 profit growth rate of Food Company Ltd against the 2017 Food Index growth rate, use a period of time, that is, a 3- or 5-year period. This means

that the average growth rate of Food Company Ltd would be compared to the average growth rate of the index.

- **Use a "constant performer" counter system to determine the best of the best**. The following example highlights the best performers for investor Robertson. Remember that this is the random approach and does not take a multitude of factors into account, namely track record, new acquisitions planned for the new financial year, or specific types of food industry the following companies operate under.
- Investor Robertson believes food companies will benefit from economic growth, higher purchasing power, and demutualization.
- There are 10 companies (fictitious) listed on the food sector of the NYSE.
- The growth performances for the last 3 years of trading of these 10 companies is outlined as follows:

| Companies and index (% growth on previous year) | | Year 1 | Year 2 | Year 3 |
|---|---|---|---|---|
| **Index** | | **+12.0** | **+14.5** | **+16.9** |
| Companies | | | | |
| 1 | A Ltd. | +33.9 | +36.7 | +39.7 |
| 2 | JJ Ltd. | −10.0 | +10.0 | +0.8 |
| 3 | KK Ltd. | −4.0 | +3.0 | +1.5 |
| 4 | KM Ltd. | −9.0 | −12.0 | −45.0 |
| 5 | BW Ltd. | +4.2 | +5.8 | +22.5 |
| 6 | GG Ltd. | +32.7 | +21.0 | +43.0 |
| 7 | HH Ltd. | +11.9 | +14.0 | +15.5 |
| 8 | PH Ltd. | −44.4 | −11.9 | −1.0 |
| 9 | LG Ltd. | −31.0 | +18.4 | −32.0 |
| 10 | TF Ltd. | +1.1 | −9.0 | −90.0 |

Here are some investment options:

**Option 1:** Buy shares in companies that constantly achieve positive annual growth rates.

| LIST A |
| --- |
| BW Ltd. |
| A Ltd. |
| GG Ltd. |
| HH Ltd. |

**Option 2:** Buy shares in companies with positive growth only during the past 2 years? These companies could have turned problems around and could continue to perform well in future.

| LIST B |
| --- |
| JJ Ltd. |
| KK Ltd. |

**Option 3:** Buy shares in companies with rates that surpass the previous years?

| LIST C |
| --- |
| A Ltd. |
| BW Ltd. |
| HH Ltd. |

Assuming that investors want winners, which are expected to continue to perform in the future? There are a number of options:

## Conclusions

From List A: A Ltd. and HH Ltd.

- A Ltd. has outperformed the market and shown constant growth, while BW Ltd. may have performed well, but the question remains whether the past year was an aberration and more history is needed before an investment decision can be made. GG Ltd. has outperformed the market, but growth is erratic and it too needs to prove itself to investors. HH Ltd. has shown constant growth over 3 years and its average rate is close to the sector growth rates. From List B: None.

- JJ Ltd. is too erratic and KK Ltd.'s growth is far too low to be considered to be a viable investment option.

From List C: A Ltd. and HH Ltd.

- A Ltd. and HH Ltd. prove themselves again.

So, from three preset options, two companies, A Ltd. and HH Ltd., appear. In this case, the investor has shown that two companies have the high probability of future growth success and are thus the best options for the investor.

## Track Records and Other factors

If management skills add value, can past performance give an indication of how these directors will perform in future? How successful will investors be if they only buy shares with the best past 3-year track record?

There is no guarantee directors will repeat past performances, nor is there a certainty the company will continue to outperform the index. It is up to the investor to keep personal records of directors' performance during the financial year.

### *Winners Often Keep Winning*

In an efficient market, it would be difficult for the same winners to keep winning, as investors have a multitude of choice and can become extremely particular in their investment decisions. Yet, over two year periods, shares that rise in price tend to repeat such trends.

Many portfolio managers suggest that chasing last year's winner does nothing more than position your portfolio with next year's potential loser. After all, it is easy enough to pick last year's winner, but not so with next year's winner.

**Chapter 11 is the start of the establishment of your portfolio rules.**

# CHAPTER 11

# Market Experts

*Your analysis and opinion matter. Following a crowd gets you average returns.*

## Portfolio Managers

**Definition:** Portfolio managers invest and manage pension and mutual funds that have been invested into equities according to a predetermined strategy.

At least, the preceding is the normal definition. In today's globalized world, portfolio managers are also employed by smaller stockbrokers, have access to investing across borders, and trade in equities and derivatives.

In many countries, portfolio managers have significant influence over the equities market. If their portfolios equate to $1billion, then imagine how much in dividend income these portfolios will earn? Where do you think those funds are invested?

When looking for an active portfolio manager to look after your funds, ensure that they can conduct research effectively and not simply follow the crowd of analysts, and make sure that they have the authority to trade on your behalf and do not simply lump your funds with everyone else's. Passive managers tend to assess various passive approaches and choose the one that suits your growth aims.

### Each with a Difference Focus

Some market experts have one track minds; either always bullish or bearish. This can ultimately be an expensive trait, as it means being wrong at the worst of times. Those that do not learn to recognize signals and adjust their portfolios accordingly do not last long in the globalized world of stock markets.

Each portfolio manager will point to reasons why their methods are the best. There is no reason why their tales may not be true. They do have some solid arguments:

- **Growth-orientated managers** assume that rapidly increasing sales, profits, and market share have to lead to a rapidly growing share price.
- **Value managers** argue that it is important to find companies that have significantly higher net asset values than share prices. These overlook companies that should provide steady growth, while high dividends and a large asset base will ensure downside protection.
- **Small company managers** believe that the next Microsoft or Anglo American will be found among the penny shares.
- **Large company managers** believe that a true investment portfolio lies securely with blue chips and second liners. Anything else is speculative and should not be worth considering.
- **Midsized company investors** strongly argue that second-tier companies offer stability, growth potential and the opportunity to exploit market inefficiencies.
- Under globalization, some managers believe that the only option open to investors is forex-hedged shares.

All these arguments do, in fact, have strong merits. However, when questioned about ethics, work methodologies and accountability, investors will discover that many managers lack common stock market or accounting definitions, often do not have appropriate yardsticks, and (in numerous instances) do not have the necessary technical tools to measure performance or risk. This does not mean these managers do not achieve acceptable and positive results.

Essentially, it is up to you to decide which type of manager you want—if you want one. These experts use different skills, timeframes, quantity of funds, and even different management techniques, which are mostly recognized and accepted worldwide.

The truth is, all these experts are competing in ruthlessly changing and volatile stock markets around the world. This often leads to advisors not telling an investor enough (in cold, hard fact) about how they achieve their results. In a competitive world, after all, telling could be giving secrets away.

The answer is, therefore, for the investors to have their own set of prerequisites. If the manager accepts these, stipulate them in writing. If the manager does not accept the prerequisites, find another manager.

Here are some prerequisites that the investor should make:

- Stipulate the type of shares (sectors) you wish to have in the portfolio.
- Always keep share certificates in your control (this is for a long-term portfolio).
- Make absolutely sure the manager does not have carte blanche to trade your portfolio.
- Stipulate degrees of buy or sell orders, that is, "if a share falls by 10 percent call me to get permission to sell or buy."

In a globalized and electronic world, you should make change your strategy and rather appoint a mentor to teach you to trade effectively and use online brokerages to conduct your own trades.

## Globalization

**Example:** Institutional portfolio managers across South Africa had a rude awakening in 1994, after the first multiparty democratic elections. In addition to having to change portfolios to reflect new local political trends, managers had to adapt to global volatility, and more hostile business, financial, and corporate trends.

Many heads of investment departments admit that many of the old rules no longer apply. For instance, prior to the 1994 election, there seemed to be a business brotherhood, in partnership with government. Analysts knew that certain contracts often went to specific companies. Now, a general consensus is that, to survive in the new South Africa, market experts will have to become more street wise and understand politics.

Politics will continue to dominate markets for a long time; not just in South Africa, but all around the world. The implication is that new governments are not bound to the old order's methods of handling political, economic, financial, and business issues and that they often have very different priorities.

While it is understood that institutions are not traders in the sense that they normally take short-term views, there is a desperate need for many global financial houses to move in line with international trends. That is, managers must be able to adapt to the clients' needs. If clients want to speculate in the market or if they want secure, long-term slow and steady growth, a portfolio manager should be able to construct a portfolio to meet these needs.

The next step, therefore, is to ascertain whether a portfolio manager can actually undertake promises made or do they make promises just to get business. Some do, others don't. The next section looks at how to avoid pitfalls in selecting a portfolio manager.

## Adopt a Cynical Approach

Who does the investor choose to run in a portfolio? The first obvious consideration is to only use institutions of sound reputation and financial solvency. Do not add additional risk by being attracted to that extra 0.5 percent promised income.

Investors must also avoid funds that promise high turnover, high expenses, high minimum investment amounts, or annual account charges.

It goes without saying that an investor should expect his advisor to have an in-depth knowledge of finance, but there is no harm in questioning him about qualifications and investment philosophy. Test him out—ask questions and then, ask him some more. The following is a list of questions that are aimed at seeing the ability of the manager to answer quickly and expertly. If the investor is a beginner, he or she should ask the advisor to explain these terms to him.

### Get Organized

When you're single, saving seems easy and budgeting even easier. However, when marriage and children come along, the odds of keeping to a budget become more difficult. Obviously, the more people in a family or

| Here Are a Number of Simple Questions |
| --- |
| • How would you use Modern Portfolio Theory to reduce risk? |
| • How much foreign exposure would you recommend? |
| • Do you believe in diversifying into emerging markets? |
| • How do you view the growth versus value debate? |
| • What do you think about market timing? |
| • How much diversification do you think is essential? |
| • What are the limitations of CAPM (discussed in later chapters)? |
| • What particular asset allocation plan do you recommend that will most likely meet my needs? |
| • How do you measure correlation between asset classes? |
| **If the investor suspects that the advisor's knowledge consists of only jargon, walk out. The important thing is to know what questions to ask and never be intimidated.** |

group of investors, for that matter, the more views and differences there are bound to be on how to budget or invest.

This brings into play the question of investing in the stock market for your children or placing funds in a bank and enjoying the benefits of the magic of compounding. It looks like magic because rather than increasing in a straight line, compounding investments increase geometrically.

Not only does the principal investment increase each year, but this year's earnings become next year's principal and accrue even more earnings. The process repeats as long as the money is left to grow. As a result, what seem like small differences in input generates giant differences. In other words, what appears to be a small change in rate of return, or slightly longer time period, will make the difference between poverty and comfort in your and your children's old age.

Before you start any long-term investment plan, get your basic financial house in order. No one should invest until they have at least a 6-month cash reserve for emergencies, the proper insurance protection and the basic legal documents. Emergencies can include unexpected hospital bills, property damage, and even retrenchment. It will not do you or your family any good to get a 30 percent rate of return if you lose your job, wreck your car, die, or get disabled tomorrow. In a very real sense, life and disability insurance buy you time.

**Chapter 12 is valuable for the novice trader, setting out lessons from the past.**

# CHAPTER 12

# Markowitz and Trading Wisdoms

*Never be a bull or bear because it's fashionable. Trades are based on fundamentals and technicals——not popular rumors.*

Harry Markowitz received the Nobel Prize for economics for his theories of modern portfolio tactics, which highlight new and better methods of controlling risk. In his Modern Portfolio Theory (MPT) he starts out by **assuming all investors are risk averse** and defines risk as a standard deviation of expected returns.

I studied Markowitz's theories in great depth back in the early 2000s and came to the conclusion that the difference between his thinking and previous other portfolio theories is he believed that, instead of measuring risk for a specific share, risk should be measured at the portfolio level.

**Therefore, each individual investment should not be examined on the basis of its individual risk, but on the contribution it makes to the entire portfolio.**

Markowitz also believed it is important to assess how investments can be expected to move together or, said differently, how investments correlate to one another. Today, many portfolio managers use his portfolio techniques for asset classes instead of individual stocks; thus constructing globally diversified portfolios.

At the risk of sounding presumptuous, I believe that traders need to take that theory and enhance it by one additional step. Traders should assess both individual shares and the portfolio as a whole.

In essence, if a single position falls below a stop loss, do you sell that stock if the overall portfolio is still substantially up? Keep this in mind as we draft the three portfolios of professional traders.

Over the past 30 years, research techniques and portfolio management systems have changed radically. If traders are to survive in a globalized and electronic world, and soon to become 24 hours a day trading exchanges, it is important to understand the influence of globalization on portfolios and also a few basic concepts from the past.

**A quick note on some key globalization points influencing traders:**

- Capitalism and free markets are the greatest wealth-creating mechanisms ever devised and stock markets adopt this stance to economics.
- As entrepreneurs and traders go about serving their own interests, the value of the world's economy increases.
- Markets, which are an integral part of capitalism, rise to reflect the increase in the world's economy.
- This trend is expected to continue.
- Markets offer all investors and traders the best opportunity to participate in the growth of the global economy.
- Risk should not be avoided, because it offers traders opportunities to participate in new companies, aiding them to grow and thus offer higher returns.
- Equities offer investors the highest real returns over time.
- Most investors and traders cannot expect to meet their reasonable goals without accepting some level of market risk.
- The impact of market timing and individual security selection pale by comparison to asset allocation and strategy.
- Risk can be actively managed.
- Diversification is the primary protection for traders and investors alike.
- Asset allocation between shares, bonds, cash, and derivatives allow investors and traders to tailor portfolios to meet their risk tolerance.
- MPT offers investors and traders the chance to attain efficient portfolios that maximize their returns for each level of risk which they are able to bear.
- Investors must accept and expect reasonably regular market declines, which are natural.

- It is vital traders maintain a long-term perspective and exercise discipline with every trade they make.
- Markets are efficient and attempts to time the market have not been effective or reliable methods of enhancing returns or reducing risk.
- Active management cannot demonstrate sufficient value add to offset their increased costs.
- The world economy is expanding, but the world's stock markets will continue to be an efficient mechanism to capture this growth in securities' value.
- Past performance of investment managers is not a reliable indicator of expected future performance.
- Cost is a controllable variable in investment management. Low cost is strongly correlated to higher investment returns. Management fees, transaction costs, and taxes all serve to reduce investor return. Costs must be rigidly controlled.

## Portfolio Lessons from the Past

### Lesson 1: Portfolio versus Economics

- Traders operate in a world that is continually changing and must thus accept that few variables are under their control if they are to succeed.
- Economists often precede forecasts with *"all things being equal,"* which means their forecasts are based on variables not changing in the near future. Traders have to adopt the opposite stance using a phrase like *"having taken numerous possible risks into account etc."* Changing variables does not mean that you cannot develop a sound, long-term strategy to build a portfolio.
- In essence, a sound strategy is one that assesses risk and rewards to maximize returns, which, over time, helps build skills and experience. When you start a portfolio, you will make mistakes until you learn your lessons.

## *Lesson 2: Equities Are Sound Investments*

- While many countries' exchanges enable traders to invest across borders, many traders have not changed their local asset allocations to a global asset allocation. This is a long-term strategy in which traders divide their available wealth among the world's desirable asset classes.
- The first task is to decide on which assets to include or exclude.
- The last 20 years have been good to equities globally, but political risk has played a major role in converting many traders into speculators. During this period, there was low inflation, high inflation, booms, recessions and depressions, high and low interest rates, war, civil unrest, and violent natural disasters. Currencies around the world were weak, then strong and stock markets around the globe boomed and crashed several times during this period (see annexures). In short, traders had plenty to worry about when going through these times, but also plenty of opportunities to trade securities.
- This period has seen portfolios change and today's investment structures are designed with the leading edge of financial and market research. However, traders should continually assess new and possibly better investment and portfolio tactics. As new tools are developed, these will usually first be available to large institutions and investment advisors, but it is only a matter of time before they are available at local retailers.

## *Lesson 3: Numbers Can Be Deceiving*

- Traders and investors alike must be conditioned to think of market timing, stock selection, and portfolio performance as fundamental keys to success. These beliefs are often deeply ingrained in novice traders, who are afraid of even superior investment returns in a strategic global asset allocation, so it will take some time for these voices to get used to global trading.

- Traders should be aware that globalization necessitates a radical change in the way portfolio managers and traders operate. For instance, investment advisors are expected to have an opinion on where the market is going and, therefore, investors and traders look to these "experts" for advice. The problem is that the market is saturated with financial experts.

- Through the media, investors are exposed daily to countless different opinions about the market, trends, and recommendations. They tell investors to retreat to the safety of cash or gold, which allows these experts to look responsible and conservative. In addition, often the first question people will ask is: "What was your performance last year?" Those numbers become the chief yardstick to determine whether the advisor is good or bad. Very seldom will the trader ask: "What's the best trading allocation?" or "How much risk do I need to take to meet my goals?"

- In a global market, traders can diversify between countries and not only sectors. The following example highlights the problem of using growth rates as the chief yardstick:

  o Mr. D. Kennedy has $1 million invested in a newly listed company on the NYSE, called ABC Ltd. At a price of $1 a share, he owns one million shares in ABC Ltd. In the first year of operation, the company landed a multibillion dollar contract with neighboring states to set up satellite stations. By the end of the first year, the company's share has moved to $2.20 a share and Kennedy has achieved a return of 120 percent on his investment.

  o Mrs. L. George had $1 million invested in the Far East and shifted her funds to first-world markets just before the 1997 stock market crash. Her portfolio looks exceptionally bright, showing a 40-percent return on a share that climbed from $100 a share to $140 a share.

These shares show phenomenal returns. Yet both sets of figures distort the true nature of the return on these investments. Kennedy's investment return is off a low base and the longer he holds the share the worse his investment return (in percentage terms) will become.

For instance, if the share rises by another 120 cents in the next 1 year, the share will have climbed to $3.40, which is an increase of 54 percent. Another 120 cents in Year 3 will mean a share price of $4.60, which is an increase of 35 percent.

To use percentage increases as a yardstick brings its own problems. That is, off a low base the company has to continually increase earnings to achieve the same rate of capital return. This is an impossible task in the short term, but if the investor had bought the share for the long term then he or she could see the share rise to $6, which means he or she would have achieved a 500-percent rate of return.

George's investment is off a high base and a 40-percent return is substantial. However, she will be hard pressed to find another investment that will offer a 40-percent return in the next 1 year.

If the investor is told by a portfolio manager that a company's attributable profit has climbed by 30 percent, the investor must insist on the base that this percentage is made. For instance, if the company had a profit of $1 million in Year 1 and $1.3 million in Year 2, this is very different to a company that has a 30-percent growth rate of a base of $1 billion in Year 1.

If the number is in the low figures (thousands or low millions) then it can be said "the company achieved a 30-percent growth off a low base of $1 million." If the amount is in the high millions or in billions then it can be said that "the company achieved a 30-percent growth off a high base of $1 billion."

**Summary:** It is more prudent to concentrate on a portfolio's long-term potential than on short-term gains. This does not mean investors should miss out on market aberrations. Set aside portions of funds to speculate, but do not use the entire portfolio.

Without tools to evaluate risk or choose between alternative strategies, investors often feel they are left with just one number to compare performance; year-to-date or last year's performance figures are the only criteria for measurement. If investors believe those figures alone determined a successful investment plan, they should buy the previous year's top-performing unit trust and ignore market signals. Unfortunately, this approach is often the worst way to form a strategy.

### Lesson 4: Change Is the Only Constant

Building a successful investment plan to meet globalization head on will require a fundamental change in the way investors think about strategy and performance objectives. The word strategy implies a conscious effort to achieve stated goals. Their concern should be to at least meet their minimum acceptable return levels without taking excessive risk.

The way an asset-allocation is designed will determine returns for short- and long-term periods. In addition, risk and returns will be driven more by the investor's asset allocation than by individual share selection or market timing. Any asset class can and will have extended periods of significant underperformance from its long-term trend.

Similarly, there will be periods when the portfolio will outperform the market trend. Of course, investors can play it safe and stay with mutual funds or unit trusts, or they can have some risky assets in their portfolios. Why have risk-related shares?

### Lesson 5: Embrace Risk

The reason is this: When risk is measured at the portfolio level, a risky asset with a low correlation to other assets in the portfolio can actually reduce risk in the portfolio. A diversified portfolio offers much higher returns per unit of risk than does a single blue chip share.

Over the long term, investment markets and portions of markets generally sort themselves out. In the short term, it is not unusual to see a negative sloping, risk-reward line, that is, the market fell and shares underperformed relative to bonds or T-Bills. The investor with a long-term return objective must know that down (and up) swings exist, but these are always temporary and have little impact on the way to meeting your goals.

Statistically, penny shares have a higher return and risk than second liners or blue chips. For the aforementioned reasons, it is never safe to talk about a company's performance in terms of percentage rates. In the international arena, even size of companies becomes relative.

In addition, emerging nation stocks have a high return profile, but also high risk. These are primarily large growth areas, but they also fall considerably below the large first-world blue chip stocks when a crisis hits emerging markets. This was amply highlighted during the 1997 stock market crash.

**Note:** What is important is how much risk the portfolio has and that it is reasonably conservative. In addition, these volumes are about strategy, which also implies a long-term approach. Even the "best" long-term strategy will not be the best each year and since we are dealing with equities and associated risk profiles, it is important to understand that even the "best" strategy does not provide investors with a guarantee against occasional negative periods.

### *Lesson 6: Markets Do Decline*

Investors often refer to risk as "the chance of the market falling." There is no doubt that no one likes to see their shares decline in price, but if they are quality stocks, losses should ultimately turn into gains. It must be stressed that investors have to wait for the market to turn before gains are achieved. This comes only after a long-term period.

Investors also seem to have any number of mental yardsticks that they employ relentlessly either against themselves or their financial advisors during periods of underperformance. Investors not only want to outperform convertible debenture rates, but they want to do that every day. Here is a truism—not even a superior portfolio will outperform debenture rates every day or every year.

In other words, reality will rear its ugly head just when you think bull runs will continue forever. The last 30-year period has been characterized by falling interest rates, falling inflation and superior stock markets, but during this period there were also the dismal stock market corrections; see appendixes.

No one should base their planning on high returns every year. As a rule of thumb, investors should expect long-term results of about 8 to 10 percent above the inflation rate. If you do better, celebrate! Just do not base your whole strategy on attaining returns that are so much higher than normal.

### Lesson 7: Trust in Your Strategy

Investors often have one more mental yardstick for comparison. The temptation to second guess yourself or your strategy is enormous. Investors are, after all, only human, and they believe, quite reasonably, that they should have it all.

Investors often tend to narrowly focus on any yardstick that is exceeding their portfolio performance for the moment. Unless investors can focus on their own goals, risk tolerance and strategy, performance becomes an impossible moving target. Investors must understand that a superior portfolio will underperform from time to time, no matter what mental yardstick they are using.

### Lesson 8: Tailor Make Your Portfolio

Investors who desire higher risks and rewards can reduce the proportion of bonds in their portfolio. Once they get to zero bonds they have two potential courses to follow if they still want higher returns.

- First, they could shift the asset allocation to more value and small company stocks.
- Second, include emerging market stocks in their portfolio.

### Lesson 9: Survival of the Fittest

There are a number of survival lessons, which are described as follows:

- **Do not do totally insane things with your money.** The Orange County disaster in the United States was the perfect example. Part of the portfolio was a derivative investment that underpinned how investors can make irrational decisions.
- **Never borrow short and lend long**. In fact, you should not borrow to make investments. Borrowing multiplies your risk.

If you borrow $1,000 to buy $2,000 worth of stock, then you will double your original money (minus interest charges) if the stock rises by 50 percent. However, you will lose your entire stake if the stock falls by 50 percent.

- **Make appropriate investments.** A consultant must always be with a legally recognized stockbroker or institution. In addition, it is important to continually check your own finances and figures—never take anything at face value.
- **Never have a preconceived scenario and fall in love with it**. Never have an absolutely unshakeable belief that economic variable will move your way, that interest rates would continue to fall, and that shares will always be positive or negative.
- **Never implement a strategy without an exit window.** When providing a portfolio manager with an order to buy or sell shares, make sure there is a stop-loss technique, that is, always set a definite price (say, 20 percent below cost) for a sell order.
- **Do not buy anything you don't understand.** If you do not understand future, commodity trading, warrants, derivatives or bonds—stay out!
- **Don't judge an investment simply by its track record**. Some companies produce spectacular returns in the first 2 years of operation, but run into problems later on. The key for an investor is not merely to look at what has been done in the past, but to understand why the company has been so successful.
- **In the market, no good thing lasts forever.** This has been said many times, if you touch hot investments, you could get burned.
- **Believe in amateur stock market sayings and see your portfolio die**. These include:
  - Knowing which stocks to buy and when to be in the market is the key to investment success.
  - A good investor can predict which way the market is going and which stocks will profit the most.
  - This power is held by just a few wise men.

o These wise men will readily share their power with you for a nominal cost.

o Knowing when the market will fall is a prime concern to the successful investor.

o One should leave the market when it is about to go down in order to preserve one's principal investment, that is, the capital amount.

o Successful investors trade often and dart in and out of the market or a particular stock with uncanny skill.

o Their portfolios benefit from a hands-on approach.

o It is easy to spot good companies through an examination of financial data and to determine what the stock in those companies should be worth.

o An astute investor can apply superior insight to make big killings on underpriced stocks. Using his superior insight he or she will be able to take action long before other investors catch on.

o Studying past price movements is an aid to predicting future price movements. This skill can be applied to both individual stocks and the movement of the market as a whole.

o Economic predictions are reliable and form another strong foundation for success. It is reasonably easy to select good advisors and managers, because their past track record is a reliable indicator of future success and skill.

Given all that, many investors tend to think of the investment process in the following terms:

- What shares should I buy?
- Should I be in or out of the market now?
- When should I sell my stocks?
- Which manager should I hire? Or, what mutual fund should I buy?
- **Unfortunately, almost all of this conventional wisdom is wrong**. It does not do us any good to think of investing in

these terms. In fact, it creates problems and keeps us away from enjoying the fruits of a game strongly tilted in our favor.

**Chapter 13 investigates and highlights traditional portfolio theory.**

# CHAPTER 13

# Traditional Portfolio Theory

*Successful traders take advantage of all market conditions; know when to go long and when to short a stock.*

It is well known in the stockbroking fraternity that of all stock exchange-related careers, the portfolio manager has the quickest burn-out period. Every day the manager faces the daunting task of providing personal attention to a multitude of clients, maintaining portfolio strengths and growth under stressful economic and political conditions, attending to general correspondence, reading volumes of market research, and actively seeking new business.

In addition, he or she has to make their own judgments on shares that are not researched by analysts. In essence, he or she is expected to know how to analyze companies and market trends within which these companies trade, has to take fundamental and technical factors into consideration, and then put his or her money where his or her mouth is and trade the shares.

There is a saying in stockbroking that there is no skill in buying or selling shares during strong bull or bear markets, but that it takes courage to go against mass hysteria and buy when others are selling.

Although this statement is relatively simple—to outperform the market the investor has to anticipate future price movements—portfolio managers have difficulty in convincing investors to hand over their cash when share prices seem to be falling down a bottomless pit.

While it may seem obvious that shareholders have a fear of buying shares during adverse conditions, the real problem stems from a lack of understanding of the theories of portfolio management.

There is thus a twofold objective in highlighting the foundations of portfolio management.

- First, to demonstrate that the core of investment knowledge is rapidly expanding.
- Second, this core is proportional to the standard of investment advice given to investors.

In other words, all investment decisions involve making a trade-off between the level of risk acceptable to the client and expected returns, since higher risks usually accompany greater returns. The manager must decide how much additional return is necessary to compensate the client for assuming greater risk.

From the earliest days of development, theories and work study on portfolio management have shown that there is one common element that is inextricably linked to success.

**If a manager is able to easily understand and control the risk variable, the greater the chances are of his achieving and maintaining strong growth.**

Although various ideas on risk management have been propagated, it is generally accepted that there are two different types, the first uncontrollable, the second controllable through technique.

## Constructing an Efficient Portfolio

I was once asked what qualities I believed were important to succeed in such a stressful environment. Ultimately, the manager who is able to remain calm and keep clients happy, while all hell is breaking loose around him, should achieve rapid success.

I was attempting to emphasize that clients tend to panic when the market underwent a temporary correction or they demand that shares be sold merely on unfounded negative rumor.

Therefore, to construct an efficient portfolio, it is necessary to have both technical structural rules to reduce risk exposure and also rules that relate to trading—that is, personal rules to remove emotion. An example of such a rule would be to sell shares if they fall by a predetermined percentage.

I have stated that portfolios are affected by systematic and unsystematic risk and that the latter can be minimized through diversification. In the following text, the former risk is evaluated and it is shown how the investor can reduce its effect on portfolios through efficient construction.

These methods are outlined as follows:

## The Efficient Frontier Model

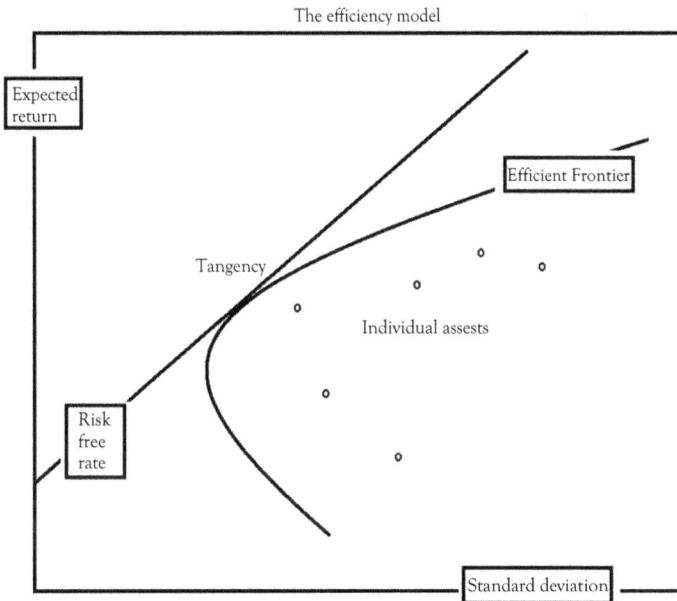

The previous diagram was developed by Harry Markowitz in 1952, which ultimately became the thrust of modern portfolio theory.

Let's break this down to make it understandable.

The diagram represents a combination of assets, whether stocks or derivatives or a combination of these, that forms a portfolio. If this portfolio of assets is devised to obtain the maximum expected level of return for a specified level of risk, then it can be said that it is efficient. The risk is represented by the standard deviation line in the diagram.

If you cannot hold risk-free assets, the upward-sloped top boundary of this region is a portion of a parabola and is called the "efficient frontier." All portfolios to the right of the tangency point are generated by borrowing at the risk-free rate and investing the proceeds into the tangency portfolio.

Economic theory describes the efficient frontier as a "theory to do with forward-looking risk and forward-looking returns." Analysis shows that it is important not to associate the theory with the implementation. Managers often use historic data to project future risk and returns, while these two factors are mutually exclusive.

It states that, for an asset or portfolio of assets to be considered efficient, no other similar portfolio can offer a higher expected return with the same risk or same return with lower risk. This is one of the main reasons that it is ultimately more efficient for a shareholder to create and maintain his own portfolio, as this will be unique and not just one of a stockbroker's mass of clients.

This model is based on five assumptions:

- Traders and investors must assess each investment and their alternatives on expected returns for a predetermined period.
- Investors want to maximize growth.
- Investors estimate risk on the basis of comparable returns and associated risk.
- The next assumption shows that investors base decisions solely on expected risks and returns.
- Finally, that they are averse to any form of risk.

### Asset Allocation

An important task of stock exchange analysts is to regularly reassess areas of the market that offer profitable investment opportunities. They are advising investors on how much money (in percentage terms) to place in equities, gold, other minerals, property, or to keep in cash until the market becomes more favorable.

This is called asset allocation and is used by investment managers to determine the current efficiency of their clients' portfolios. Some managers believe that stocks and other securities are not the only assets which should be allocated. They say the investors' motor vehicles, house, antiques, furniture, and so on should also be assessed. These show what the investors' intentions, objectives, and constraints are.

These three volumes suggest that an asset allocation can be made up as follows:

- **Never more than two stocks per sector**, until you have at least three sectors covered.
- **Keep mostly to shares that are $10 and above**. This is a sound starting point for beginners and enables the investor to acquire larger amounts of shares at the beginning of his long-term plans.
- **Keep at least 5 percent of a portfolio in cash**, for opportunities that come up, that is, not speculative.
- **Keep 5 percent of the portfolio in speculative stocks**. Even if a new speculative opportunity comes, keep to that 5 percent limit.
- **Diversify across various sectors**, that is, between financial, mining, and consumer stocks.
- **Each share must be analyzed before purchased**, unless it forms part of the speculative portion of the portfolio.
- **Keep a limit on the number of shares in the portfolio**. Remember that the more shares that comprise the portfolio, the more time consuming analysis becomes and maintaining financial efficiency could become a full-time job.
- **Limit downside by having a stop-loss philosophy.** Remove emotion from trading by selling any share—no matter the reason—if it falls by a level that makes you uncomfortable. Therefore, if a 15-percent drop in the share price makes you uncomfortable, take your loss by selling the share, even if you strongly believe that the share will recover.
- **Take profits regularly.** Similar to the stop-loss philosophy, sell a share that rises by a certain amount. This places cash in your portfolio and enables you to buy another potential winner. However, regularly review the portfolio and return the percentage level of share that has climbed back to zero. This enables you to plan a long-term growth strategy per share and also for the portfolio as a whole.

# Asset Allocation for the Conservative, Moderate, or Aggressive Investor

The following are portfolio asset allocation suggestions and includes foreign investment.

Note that these are suggested allocations and every individual should structure their portfolios in a manner that enables them to feel comfortable. The following portfolio allocations use a timeframe of 3, 10, and 30 years. These portfolios are based on the categories outlined in the following.

### Different Portfolio Security-Types

- **Aggressive shares:** Capital appreciation funds, venture capital shares, emerging market shares, specific global funds, and shares.
- **Conservative shares:** Growth and income unit trusts, blue chip shares (first-world countries) and conservative growth funds.
- **Fixed income:** Long-term convertible debentures and long bonds.
- **Hybrids:** Balanced funds, asset allocation funds, high yield gilts, equity income funds, global bonds, and emerging country debt funds.
- **Cash:** Money market funds, liquid savings accounts (cash in the bank), and short-term convertible debentures.

**The following portfolios represent the norm for conservative, moderate, and aggressive investors. In later volumes we set out portfolios for professional traders:**

| Types of securities (figures in %) | The Short-Term Portfolio (3 years) | | |
|---|---|---|---|
| | Types of Investors | | |
| | Conservative | Moderate | Aggressive |
| Conservative shares | 25 | 20 | 10 |
| Fixed income securities | 40 | 40 | 40 |
| Aggressive shares | 0 | 10 | 30 |
| Cash | 30 | 20 | 5 |
| Hybrids | 5 | 10 | 15 |
| TOTAL | 100 | 100 | 100 |

| Types of securities (figures in %) | The Long-Term Portfolio (10 years) | | |
|---|---|---|---|
| | Types of Investors | | |
| | Conservative | Moderate | Aggressive |
| Conservative | 25 | 20 | 5 |
| Fixed income securities | 30 | 30 | 20 |
| Aggressive stocks | 20 | 20 | 50 |
| Cash | 15 | 15 | 5 |
| Hybrids | 10 | 15 | 20 |
| TOTAL | 100 | 100 | 100 |

| Types of securities (figures in %) | The Life-Time Portfolio (30 years) | | |
|---|---|---|---|
| | Types of Investors | | |
| | Conservative | Moderate | Aggressive |
| Conservative | 25 | 20 | 5 |
| Fixed income securities | 25 | 20 | 10 |
| Aggressive stocks | 30 | 50 | 70 |
| Cash | 10 | 0 | 5 |
| Hybrids | 10 | 10 | 10 |
| TOTAL | 100 | 100 | 100 |

- The longer the portfolio time horizon, the less cash-type securities are in portfolios of any kind.
- **Even the most conservative investor holds very little cash**, but he or she does hold a large portion of funds in fixed income securities.
- **The shorter the time span, the higher the risk of investing.** Therefore, even the aggressive investor, who is seeking to maximize profits as quickly as possible, holds conservative shares and fixed income securities.
- The investor must **keep a long-term goal firmly in mind** while having the flexibility to evolve as new research provides better solutions to the risk management problem or new market opportunities present themselves.
- **Discipline remains the key to success for long-term investors**, that is, falling into a panic trap of selling during bear markets or buying during strong bull markets.

- **A successful investment strategy involves patience, discipline, and periodic reviews** that must be viewed as an opportunity for fine tuning and occasional modest course corrections, not radical revision and second guessing.

## The Capital Asset Pricing Model (CAPM)

This model establishes the inherent risk of an individual share on the whole portfolio. It is calculated through a complex formula, which incorporates the expected rate of return of the share, interest rate, and the expected average rate of return on all shares in the economy.

This model is used to determine the expected return of a share. The manager calculates the net present value of a number of shares, which provides him with a number of investment options. However, there is a difference of opinion among managers as to the accuracy of the CAPM, which has led to further research for more acceptable alternatives. Managers say that the problem in using the CAPM is that, while there is a definite relationship between rates of return and systematic risk for complete portfolios, none exists for individual shares.

## The Arbitrage Pricing Theory (APT)

This theory was first outlined by SA Ross in his book "Economic forces and the stock market," (published 1986) and is based on three assumptions.

- First, capital markets are perfectly competitive.
- Second, investors prefer more to less wealth.
- Third, the process of generating asset returns can be represented in a model.

He believed that investors were able to avoid unsystematic risk. The main importance in using the APT model is that it does not rely on a true market portfolio and is, thus, a more realistic aid to managers in assessing efficient portfolios.

In essence, these theories show that the investor has to determine his risk tolerance and measure this against his expected returns.

# Bring It All Together

A better benchmark can be created for just about any market or portion of a market.

For example, suppose we divided all the publicly listed stocks in the NYSE into 10 different sizes by market capitalization on one axis, and 10 different segments based on debt and equity ratio on the other axis. We now have 100 different possible submarkets. We could call each submarket an investment style and each style could have its own index or benchmark.

If we studied the performance of each style, we would find they are sharply different from each other. Each style would have distinctly separate identities. For instance:

- Rates of return could vary substantially between the submarkets.
- These submarkets could exhibit different risk or standard deviations.
- Each could also have a different correlation from the other.
- Each style could go through a market cycle with dramatically different results for each time period.

# Conclusions

- There is not just one domestic market, but many.
- Many portfolio managers confine themselves to a distinct market segment. For instance, they may be large-cap value, midcap growth, or small-cap market. This is the area of the market they claim to know best and believe has the greatest potential. In any event, over time most of the performance they obtain may simply be attributable to where in the market they invest.
- Investors can therefore design precise benchmarks.
- The investment style of portfolio managers around the world has become more important than management prowess.
- Even when a director beats his competitors, investors cannot be sure growth was a direct consequence of the director's ability, right market conditions, or just dumb luck.

Even within a carefully defined style, investors are still faced with a wide variation of results in both the short and long terms. Part of this is attributable to style differences within the markets, but a large amount of variation can also be attributed to sector or "window dressing" by portfolio managers.

Many stock markets' majority of shares are owned by large institutions, which means the weight of funds at their disposal can (and often does) move share prices. Window dressing is a term used when portfolio managers buy shares to boost the performance of their portfolios.

### Example

The following example assumes that new portfolio manager Robert has set up a portfolio, which shows no capital growth.

- Robert has 10,000 shares in ABC Ltd.
- He bought these at $100 each.
- The value of his portfolio is therefore $1 million.
- If he uses the institution's weight of funds to buy 10,000 more ABC Ltd. shares, which are difficult to obtain (called tightly traded shares), the net worth of his portfolio could rise.

Assuming that Robert was able to buy 10,000 more ABC Ltd. shares at an average price of $130 a share, the value of his portfolio rises to 20,000 shares at $130 a share. Remember that the original shares are now also worth $130 a share. In essence, he has made a net profit from buying more expensive shares.

**Cost of Robert acquiring ABC Ltd. shares:**

| Shares | Price | Value |
|---|---|---|
| 10,000 shares | at $100 | $1,000,000 |
| 10,000 shares | at $130 | $1,300,000 |
| Total cost | | $2,300,000 |

**Value of Robert's portfolio:**

| Shares in ABC Ltd | Quantity | Share Price | Value |
|---|---|---|---|
| Original shares held | 10,000 | $100 | $1,000,000 |
| Shares bought | 10,000 | $130 | $1,300,000 |
| Total shares held | 20,000 | $130 | $2,600,000 |

**Profit made by increasing the portfolio:**

| Profit | = | Total value of shares | – | Cost of shares |
|---|---|---|---|---|
| | = | $2.6 million | – | $2.3 million |
| | = | $300,000 | | |
| | = | 13% increase in value of the portfolio | | |

When investors build investment strategies, a benchmark, style, or passive approach may be very viable. After all, what's wrong with top-quartile results of unit trusts? All other things being equal, when given a choice between actively managed funds, investors should opt for the one with the lowest cost, widest diversification, and lowest turnover.

In fact, investors have actually returned to the thesis that asset allocation is much more important than focusing on a particular share, timing, or directors' performance. In fact, there are mathematical methods of assessing a director's ability.

**Chapter 14 establishes your ultimate portfolio.**

# CHAPTER 14

# Steps to the Ultimate Portfolio

*The true art of stupidity is to sell trades that show a profit and keep those that show a loss.*

There are effectively as many steps as there are different types of risks. I suggest the following diagram as an example of the time span that it takes the investor to understand the various elements that make up a sound portfolio. Therefore, once the investor has a sound knowledge of the following, he or she is ready to start trading:

- A sound understanding of the investment environment.
- Understands the mechanics of buying and selling shares.
- Has a firm grasp of portfolio-related risk factors, asset allocation, and methodologies.

I suggest a threefold approach to the creation of an investment portfolio.

- **Start small, with low-risk investments** for a period of at least 2 years. This will give the investor or trader time to get to understand how markets operate, factors that drive shares, and get that gut feel that makes the investor more street wise.
- **Move into medium-risk investments**. Here, I suggest indexing.
- After a period of 3 to 5 years, the investor can start **combining shares with other investment alternatives.**

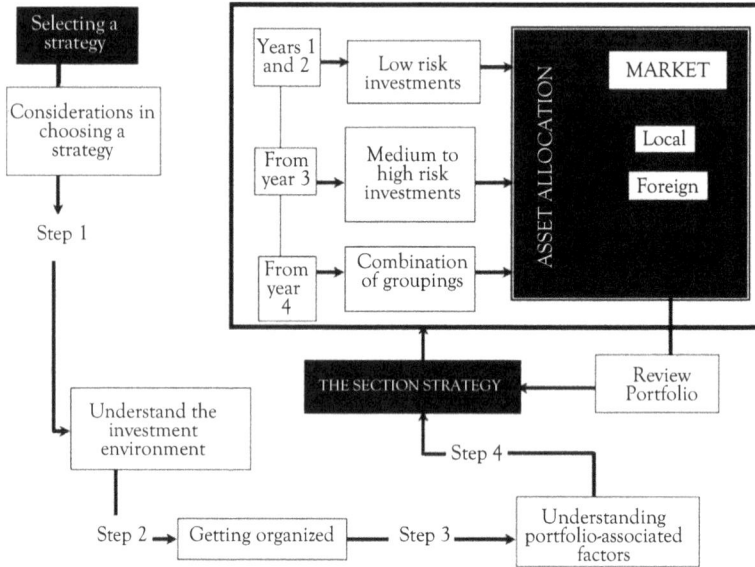

### Your Starting Point

The unit trust industry is a sound way to build up a relatively liquid portfolio, which can be cashed in after 2 years to start the share selection. In addition, this industry has been very successful in getting their message across. Traditionally, investors have thought of diversification, low cost, and access to strong management as the chief advantages of unit trusts.

The first two are true: Where else can an investor buy a portfolio containing hundreds of individual issues across a market with as little as $1,000? In addition, the fee structure is moderate and not crippling. The small investor thus has a chance to set up a portfolio and accumulate wealth.

However, if the investor does not believe that unit trust managers can add value, they can invest in index or passively managed funds. As designers of a superior investment strategy based on strategic global asset allocation, investors should select unit trusts that allow them to very tightly control their portfolio.

Unit trusts are gaining market share, because they are a better investment medium for the small investor to start a portfolio. However, it must be stressed that "start" is the operative word. Once investors have enough funds to move directly into the market, they should do so.

How does the unit trust industry work? Once understood, the investor can develop a few simple criteria to drive their selection decisions. This procedure is fairly straightforward and it allows you to gain control of the total investment process.

## Unit Trusts

- General equity funds that invest in a wide range of shares. This is the perfect starting point for an investment strategy as they are established, have a lower risk, and provide a broad-based knowledge of stock market movements.
- Index funds can be used as the second step in the strategy, that is, before moving to index stocks, use index unit trusts to build knowledge of the index stocks. These unit trusts strive to track the performance of a targeted index.
- Specialist equity funds, which concentrate on specific types of shares, that is, mining, gold, financial, and industrial funds.
- Specific funds which invest in various specified market sectors. The investor can build up knowledge of sectors before moving into the stock market.
- Smaller company funds that can be used to boost the percentage growth of the portfolio.
- Income funds are invested in interest-bearing securities such as gilts.
- Managed funds, which offer a mix of the aforementioned types of funds, that is, equities, fixed-interest assets, and property.

It does not have to be perfect to be great. Get started. Do not wait for it to be perfect. It never will be and you will still be waiting when you are old and broke. The important thing is to get started on a sensible plan and exercise the discipline to carry it out. Start small and build over time. If the choices are not perfect, do the best you can.

### Switch to Index Stocks

Once the investor has become familiar with share movements (using unit trusts), the next step in performance monitoring is to build an asset allocation plan portfolio using only index stocks.

This is the start of building a real understanding of how shares work. It will help the investor understand the total performance of a portfolio and put it in perspective. There is, however, no difference in the mechanics of running an index stock portfolio to a unit trust portfolio.

During any form of portfolio review, the investor should strenuously resist the temptation to replace a disappointing fund with the latest fashion shares. Continually changing a portfolio is unlikely to improve performance and will result in a losing strategy. It is crucial to understand that fund evaluation and performance monitoring are tactical in nature.

An asset allocation plan should be changed only on the following basis:

- **New, better analytical methods become known:** When a new fundamental method of assessing shares and portfolios is promoted in the media, among analysts, and by the academia, distinguish between proven, tested, academic, industry research and complete nonsense.
- **Moving into the global arena:** When the investor moves from a domestic bound portfolio to a global one, it becomes important to understand and distinguish between:
  - First-world market, where the company invested in is bound to that specific country, that is, Company AA is listed on the London Stock Exchange and operates only in the UK.
  - First-world market, where the company invested in is listed in that country, but has operations in other markets, that is, Company AA is listed on the New York Stock Exchange and has operation divisions in other first-world or emerging markets.

### Indexing

*Indexing* simply describes an investment approach that seeks to parallel the investment returns of a specified stock market benchmark, or index. The investment manager attempts to replicate the investment results of the target index by holding all—or in the case of very large indexes, a representative sample—of the securities in the index. There is no attempt to narrow industry sectors in an attempt to outpace the index, which means that indexing is really a passive approach emphasizing broad diversification and low portfolio trading activity.

Indexing, in its simplest form, thus means buying all of the stocks (or index stocks) of a specific sector, instead of trying to pick winners and losers.

Indexing is also called "passive investing" or "asset class" investing.

## Benefits

Indexing eliminates the risks, costs, and uncertainties that are associated with actively managing a portfolio, that is, picking specific shares and picking these at the right time (market timing).

## Cost Advantages

Investors should note that indexing is really not suited to investors who have a long-term strategy to achieve realistic returns, but higher than sector or overall market averages. If markets do operate efficiently, then it is impossible for all investors in the aggregate to outperform the overall stock market.

### Comment

- Decide on a mix of active and passive techniques, that is, your aim should be 70 percent unit trust, 20 percent equities, and 10 percent cash initially.
- Once the investor has grown in confidence, develop a long-term strategy and reduce the unit trust component to around 10 percent.
- Define the market as tightly as possible, that is, large, small, foreign, emerging markets, Asia, Japan, Europe, and so on.
- Make sure the manager stays fully invested and within the assigned market.

- Define the style of companies to invest in, that is, growth versus value. (A strong value tilt should enhance performance and reduce risk.)
- Check expense ratio. (The lower, the better. Remember that, however, some markets cost more than others.)
- Check portfolio turnover. (The lower the better.)
- Compare performance to appropriate benchmark and competitive funds. Try to understand any variation from benchmark. (There is always a reason. Higher returns mean higher risk.)

### Rebalancing the Portfolio

Once an investor has developed a long-term investment strategy, it is crucial to conduct periodic rebalancing, which means bringing the asset allocation back to its original target.

To bring your portfolio back to its original, predetermined mix:

- Sell the investment that exceeds its recommended percentage and invest the proceeds in other investments.
- Add new money to the investments that are below their recommended percentage.
- In a mutual fund setting, direct dividends from the investment that exceeds its recommended percentage to the investments that are below its target allocation.

The reason that it is necessary to rebalance a portfolio is to maintain a steady allocation between the different share selections. Rebalancing should be undertaken at least once a year, although some dedicated investors adjust their portfolios monthly or quarterly.

## Adjusting Financial Plans

A long-term strategy does not imply a passive approach. Changes in life do occur and a plan to fine tune the portfolio is thus necessary. The following are examples of instances when an investor may consider changing his investment portfolio.

- **Changing careers:** Changing jobs, incomes, retirement, or an inheritance may change the focus of a long-term portfolio. The investor may want to be less conservative and more moderate or aggressive.
- **An income change:** A change in household income may lead to an adjustment in the amount earmarked for investment.
- **A family change:** A marriage, divorce, birth, or death could also have profound, yet quite different, effects on your investment planning, and may necessitate a review of your investment strategy.
- **A change in monthly expenditure:** Paying off a major expense may enable an investor to reexamine his financial status. The higher disposable income may permit the investor to start (or increase) a rand-cost averaging program.
- **A change in age:** The closer to retirement an investor gets, the more important it is to reassess the portfolio on a regular basis.

**Once the investor has a sound knowledge of stock markets, investment criteria and methods of asset allocation, reducing risk profiles, and establishing a portfolio, it is time to develop a stock-picking strategy. What companies should you invest in? Where do you get information? How are companies evaluated?**

**In volume 2, we set out the basics of establishing your own trading room.**

# Appendixes

## By the Same Author

1. Share Analysis & Company Forecasting (Struik Business Library, 1995)
2. The Business Plan: A Manual for South African Entrepreneurs (Zebra Press, 1996)
3. The Millionaire Portfolio (Zebra Press, 2003)
4. Jungle Tactics: Global Research, Investment & Portfolio Strategies (Heinemann, 2003)
5. A Guide to AltX: Listing on SA's Alternative Stock Exchange (Zebra, 2004)
6. Become Your Own Stockbroker (Zebra, 2005)
7. The Corporate Mechanic: The Analytical Strategist's Guide (Juta, 2007)
8. Richer Than Buffett: Day Trading to Ultra-Wealth (Struik, 2007)
9. The Guerrilla Principle: Winning Tactics for Global Project managers (Juta, 2008)
10. Women & Wealth: Footsteps to Financial Freedom (Oshun, 2009)
11. Lore of the Global Trader (Penguin, 2011)
12. Master Trader (Penguin, 2011)
13. Business & Entrepreneurship (Milpark Business School, 2013)
14. The Penny Share Millionaire (Business Expert Press, 2017)

## Author Profile

*Jacques is an economist, corporate strategist, and advisor to multinationals and SMEs and an internationally bestselling published author, speaker, and lecturer.*

Brief Overview:

- Jacques has an economics master's degree specializing in stock markets.
- Currently pursuing his PhD in economics at the University of Stellenbosch, in South Africa.
- Has written 14 financial books. Five are university MBA textbooks.
- Corporate advisor in over 1,200 major projects since July 2000.
- Associate to Chamber of Mines and numerous stockbroking firms.
- Sits on various boards of listed and private companies
- Former director and head of research for Stockbrokers Global Capital Securities.
- Currently group CEO of corporate finance and technical research group Business Consultants International.

Jacques has been an investment and corporate strategist since 1987. He started his career as a financial journalist for the *Financial Mail*, before being headhunted into stockbroking.

Since 1987, Jacques has written for international publications (UK Petroleum Economist, Mail & Guardian, and Financial Mail) and undertaken corporate consultancy for international clients, including defense force, universities, and multinationals.

His experience thus includes stockbroking, business development, and corporate strategy. Before setting up Business Consultants International in July 2000, he was a director, strategist, and head of research for South African stockbrokers Global Capital Securities.

Business Consultants International concentrates on assisting entrepreneurs to restructure their firms to become more efficient, profitable, and compliant to the vast number of legislation critical to the success of any company. Jacques has developed a four-phase approach to corporate intelligence, which includes in-depth market research and analysis, due diligence, business plans, corporate profiles, and implementation strategies.

In addition, Jacques has also regularly been interviewed on SABC's News Today, Summit TV, and CNBC Africa.

Born in Morocco, Jacques moved to South Africa and began his career for the *Financial Mail* in 1987, before moving into stockbroking in 1990. Today Jacques lives in Cape Town with his wife Kathy and children.

## The World Federation of Stock Exchanges

The World Federation of Exchanges (WFE) is the trade association of 63 publicly regulated equities, futures, and options exchanges. Formed in 1961 and based in London, UK, the WEF is responsible for operating the key components of the global industry association for exchanges and clearing houses.

Impressively, it represents over 200 market infrastructure providers, with 41 percent of its members based in the Asia-Pacific region, 40 percent in EMEA, and 19 percent in the Americas. These comprise 45,000 listed companies, with a market capitalization of over $67.9 trillion.

## Crashes and Corrections

| Year | Title | Trading days | Cause of Crash |
|---|---|---|---|
| 1987 | Program trade | 456 | The crash came after a 5-year bull run. Wall Street fell by almost 23% in a day, while the FTSE 100 fell by 20% in 2 days. |
| 1997 | Asian crisis | 46 | The United States' increase in interest rates ultimately caused a contagion, sparking a financial crisis in Mexico, Thailand, Korea, and the Philippines. Western stock markets fell, but rebounded quickly. |
| 1998 | Russian crisis | 44 | The Asian crisis lead to commodity prices affecting Russia's foreign exchange reserves, devaluing the rouble and this triggered financial panic around the world. |
| 2000 | Tech bubble | 1,015 | At the height of investor hunger for tech stocks, IPO shares doubled on its first day of trading. The bubble burst, and was compounded by the panic induced by the 9/11 attacks on the United States. |

| 2008 | Global financial crisis | 230 | When Lehman Brothers filed for bankruptcy, the world's financial markets entered a crash. It took nearly 2 years for the index to recover. |
|---|---|---|---|
| 2011 | Greek debt crisis | 116 | A massive default on the Greek debt sparked panic, but markets recovered quickly when the European institutions and the IMF granted Greece a bailout. |
| 2015 | Black Monday | 36 | Global investors lost temporary confidence on the back of China's stock market bubble. |

**Key: trading days:** days to regain precrash level

# Index

## OTHER TITLES IN OUR FINANCE AND FINANCIAL MANAGEMENT COLLECTION

John A. Doukas, Old Dominion University, Editor

- *Designing Learning and Development for Return on Investment* by Carrie Foster
- *The Penny Share Millionaire: The Ultimate Guide to Trading* by Jacques Magliolo
- *Applied International Finance Volume I, Second Edition: Managing Foreign Exchange Risk* by Thomas J. O'Brien
- *Applied International Finance Volume II, Second Edition: International Cost of Capital and Capital Budgeting* by Thomas J. O'Brien
- *Rethinking Risk Management: Critically Examining Old Ideas and New Concepts* by Rick Nason
- *Towards a Safer World of Banking: Bank Regulation After the Subprime Crisis* by T.T. Ram Mohan
- *Escape from the Central Bank Trap: How to Escape From the $20 Trillion Monetary Expansion Unharmed* by Daniel Lacalle
- *Tips & Tricks for Excel-Based Financial Modeling: A Must for Engineers & Financial Analysts, Volume I* by M. A. Mian
- *Tips & Tricks for Excel-Based Financial Modeling: A Must for Engineers & Financial Analysts, Volume II* by M. A. Mian
- *The Anti-Bubbles: Opportunities Heading into Lehman Squared and Gold's Perfect Storm* by Diego Parrilla

# Announcing the Business Expert Press Digital Library

*Concise e-books business students need for classroom and research*

This book can also be purchased in an e-book collection by your library as

- a one-time purchase,
- that is owned forever,
- allows for simultaneous readers,
- has no restrictions on printing, and
- can be downloaded as PDFs from within the library community.

Our digital library collections are a great solution to beat the rising cost of textbooks. E-books can be loaded into their course management systems or onto students' e-book readers.
The **Business Expert Press** digital libraries are very affordable, with no obligation to buy in future years. For more information, please visit **www.businessexpertpress.com/librarians**. To set up a trial in the United States, please email **sales@businessexpertpress.com**.